William Frederic Faber

Nobiscum Deus

The gospel of the incarnation

William Frederic Faber

Nobiscum Deus
The gospel of the incarnation

ISBN/EAN: 9783741132360

Manufactured in Europe, USA, Canada, Australia, Japa

Cover: Foto ©Andreas Hilbeck / pixelio.de

Manufactured and distributed by brebook publishing software (www.brebook.com)

William Frederic Faber

Nobiscum Deus

Nobiscum Deus

THE GOSPEL
OF THE INCARNATION

BY

WILLIAM FREDERIC FABER

AUTHOR OF "THE CHURCH FOR THE TIMES"

NEW YORK
ANSON D. F. RANDOLPH AND COMPANY
(INCORPORATED)
182 FIFTH AVENUE

TO

PROFESSOR CHARLES W. SHIELDS, D.D., LL.D.,

WHOSE DEVOUT AND CATHOLIC SPIRIT HAS ENLISTED A RARE
SCHOLARSHIP AND A GIFTED PEN IN THE
SERVICE OF CHRISTIAN UNITY,

This Little Book is Gratefully Dedicated.

CONTENTS.

		PAGE
I.	THE KINGDOM OF GOD	7
II.	THE KINGDOM OF GOD WITHIN US	19
III.	THE KINGDOM OF GOD COMING ON EARTH	31
IV.	THE UNIVERSAL KINGDOM OF GOD	45
V.	GREAT JOY TO ALL PEOPLE	61
VI.	THE HUMAN LIFE DIVINE	77
VII.	PURE RELIGION	93
VIII.	THE PRICE AND THE PURCHASE	109
IX.	AN EASTER SUMMONS	125
X.	OUR ASCENDED LORD	141
XI.	THE SPIRIT OF PENTECOST	155
XII.	CONTENDING FOR THE FAITH	171

I.

The kingdom of God.

And in those days cometh John the Baptist, preaching in the wilderness of Judæa, saying, Repent ye; for the kingdom of heaven is at hand. — MATT. iii. 1, 2.

Now after that John was delivered up, Jesus came into Galilee, preaching the gospel of God, and saying, The time is fulfilled, and the kingdom of God is at hand: repent ye, and believe in the gospel. — MARK i. 14, 15.

I.

THE KINGDOM OF GOD.

OUR religious vocabulary abounds in terms which, through long and often inapt use, have lost their original distinctness and power. Like gold pieces from which image and superscription have been effaced, they must be sent back to the mint of thought to be recoined, ere they can be of full value.

An instance in point is this very familiar expression, "the kingdom of God." Few phrases have wider currency; few, we might add, have more sadly degenerated into cant. But, even where we may not justly suspect cant, where it is used with evident sincerity out of an honest heart, how far it commonly is from expressing any single, definite, and adequate idea! To put the matter to the test, take the familiar verse, St. Matthew vi. 33: "Seek ye first the kingdom of God and his righteousness, and all these things shall be added unto you." I ask the question, "In what direction shall I look for this kingdom?" There are some who will answer, "The future world; heaven." They think that the Saviour enjoins upon men to prepare for the hereafter, and He will the while care for their earthly maintenance. But though I will agree that this earth is not all, that a fuller and higher life awaits us after this present, and shall not be entered save by the pure and righteous, it seems to me that no one can read the record of John the Baptist's preaching, and of our Lord's at His first public appearance, and yet hold that the "kingdom" is postponed to another world. Others there are who, impatient of such postponement, tell us, "The kingdom of God is here; Christ established it, gave it organization and ordinances and promise of perpetuity; the kingdom of God for us here is the Church; and our first duty is to find our place within her, and take up the service of Christ in her membership." Now while we believe with all our heart in "the Holy Catholic Church," and cheerfully assent to every proper claim urged on her behalf, again it must be said that in the Gospels "Church" and "kingdom of God" cannot be taken as interchangeable. But there are still others who zealously make reply, "The kingdom of God is within you; ye must be born again; this must be your first and all-absorbing concern." Grant that rightly understood such an answer gives us the key to every God-ward and man-ward duty. The trouble is, those who most loudly assert this truth are commonly the

most superficial and mechanical interpreters of it;
a "change of heart," to use the familiar phrase,
is by them often held equivalent to character
and conduct both, when in reality it compasses
neither, but is only a surface emotionalism.
Moreover, granting the genuineness of it, the
"kingdom within you" will not suffice to cover
all which the Gospels compel us to include in the
"kingdom of God."

Satisfied that these popular conceptions, even
when they are as definite as this, give us no adequate
account of the great. Reality proclaimed
by John the Baptist and by our Blessed Lord
Himself, let us strike out for ourselves, to
reach if we may some satisfactory view of this
Kingdom.

We may say, in passing, that no reader who
will attend to the parallel accounts of St. Matthew
and St. Mark can fail to note that where
the former writes "kingdom of heaven," the latter
writes "kingdom of God." Evidently they
stand for exactly the same thing, — "heaven"
deriving all its significance from the fact of its
being viewed as the dwelling-place of God, the
realm where He is all in all. It will be sufficient,
therefore, if we study the more common phrase,
the "kingdom of God."

In one sense, the kingdom of God extends over
all the universe, for in heaven and earth He is

supreme. In that sense there is no room for the petition, "Thy kingdom come," nor for the announcement, "The kingdom is at hand." Evidently this "kingdom" which we are to seek stands not upon the Almightiness of God. May we not say that it is rather *the willing acknowledgment of His kingship, the cordial acceptance of His rule?* And looking at the matter in this light, does not God's kingship mean the enthronement of His character; does not His rule mean conformity to Himself? What, then, is that character? What is He?

Questions like these it behooves us to approach reverently, avoiding the presumptuous familiarity with which men sometimes speak of the plans and the attributes of the Almighty as though they had comprehended them all. Yet we may speak confidently. Whatever else He be beyond our ken, we know that God is *Righteousness*, and *Truth*, and *Love;* apart from qualities like these it is impossible for us to conceive of God as God at all. And the kingdom of God — whatever else it may be — is the enthronement of Righteousness, and Truth, and Love. To be in that kingdom is to be under the willing dominion of these; to own them for Master Principles, and seek them in all things more and more. As George Eliot makes Savonarola say : " Necessity is laid on me, which I dare not gainsay, to preach this Gospel of God's kingdom, as, even on earth, a kingdom of righteousness, truth, and love."

Let no one suppose that these are abstractions of the lecture-room or study. Righteousness, what is it but that fundamental *Rightness* which a soul sound at the core will see and acknowledge, yea, vehemently assert, though it were in the midst of darkness and struggle like that of Abraham? — "Shall not the Judge of all the earth do right?" Truth, what is it but that elemental *Reality* and *Genuineness* to which we are ever appealing against the shams and hollowness and insincerities of the world? — as when Carlyle cries out, "Fool! the Eternal is no simulacrum!" Love, last and best word of all, what is it but this that has left its witness in every human heart, drawing upon it like a yet undiscovered Planetary Force, left out of reckoning by Unbelief; what is it but this which opens lips unused to prayer to cry out in time of darkness and trouble to Him as to One who cares? Of which a seer sings: —

"I have gone the whole round of creation; I saw and I spoke.
 I, a work of God's hand for that purpose, received in my brain
 And pronounced on the rest of His hand work — returned Him again
 His creation's approval or censure; I spoke as I saw.
 I report, as a man may of God's work — all 's love, yet all 's law."

The kingdom of such a God we may well expect to be no mere name, or theory, or sentiment; but, where it has truly come, a most mighty Fact, a most Blessed Reality!

And therefore our Lord brings to men the announcement of this kingdom as a "gospel of God," a piece of good news from heaven. Through it better things were in store for all who would make ready for them. For the men of Jesus' day were looking, as men always have looked, as men are still looking, for a *better future*. To be sure, men's notions of that better future have differed infinitely. At that time and in that land they were looking for the restoration of David's throne and the recovery of their national independence and their former greatness. In other times and other lands it has been the overthrow of some hated despotism, the elevation of some class, the expansion of industry or commerce, the extension of common education, the development of letters and the arts, the perfection of legislative or judicial or executive machinery; according to their times, their training, their breadth of vision, their condition morally, intellectually, socially, industrially, they have pictured that better future under one or another to them attractive guise. History is one long succession of examples. As to external and material improvement, the desires of one generation become the attainments of the next; is the happy time brought nearer? A hundred years have witnessed what vast changes in all the conditions of man's natural life and environment! — are men as a whole happier? Is the craving satisfied, is the expectation met? Things earnestly desired in the eighteenth century, men have now, in the nineteenth; is all well? Is it a mere accident that the generation which has witnessed material invention and achievement, material expansion and progress unparalleled through the centuries, should be flooded with a literature the saddest, most depressing, disillusionizing, pessimistic? Drinking our fill of the wealth of *things*, is it strange that so many of us should begin to be sceptical as to whether there will be a better future at all, having ourselves found that increase of *things* will not bring it?

Wherein, ultimately and essentially, must the satisfactions of the better future consist? Must they not have respect to what is divinest in man, unlikest the brute; must they not be satisfactions of the *spirit?* This Jesus of Nazareth, then, whose voice men would not or could not hear because of the din they made in heralding their manifold world-improvement schemes, — has He not, perhaps, after all, the most practical way to the better future? How well we know that apart from advance in goodness no advance in the "arts of living" has ever really lifted men or made life richer to them! How well we know that increased intelligence without increased goodness has imperilled and debased peoples, rather than strengthened and exalted them! How well we know that "institutions" bestowed in hope of conferring freedom and happiness have led to precisely the opposite result when there has been no corresponding character in the recipients! Could we to-day feed every human being on the globe, house comfortably every family, set every man his fitting task with just compensation, give each his part in civic privilege, each an honorable recognition and reception in society, and to all the refining influences of libraries and art galleries with doors wide open, — and add to these whatever else from the long catalogue of "Civilization" you may choose — would in all these have come the better day for the human race? There may be those who think so; but they err. One thing, as men are, would be lacking — *character*. The arrangements might be perfect; but, while men were what they are, the arrangements could not last. Or, compelled to remain in what they were not fitted for, their misery and chagrin would but be the greater.

This Jesus, then, — does He not care for the amelioration of human existence? Food, raiment, shelter,— knowledge, beauty, social joys, and civic rights — are they nothing to him? Let us never forget that the Son of Man came eating and drinking, and that it was He who said, "Render unto Cæsar the things that are Cæsar's." We have misread His life if we suppose Him indifferent to the wrong which defrauds any human being of any rightful privilege or pleasure ; if we suppose He regards with equanimity any system or state of things which deprives any man, woman, or child of the Father's intended gifts. But He will lay the chief stress upon the chief need. He will insist upon the essential thing. He bids you seek first that which is first, the kingdom of God. He does it for your sake. He knows that nothing will supply its place, if you lack *that*. He knows that there is no surer way to supply all other needful things, no other way to give those things any value and make them afford any satisfaction, than to have, hold, and enjoy them under the kingdom of God. And this is no more true of the individual than it is of society. The only gospel for men, the only substantial promise of a really better future, is in that which Jesus preached, The Kingdom of God.

Now, all this, it scarcely needs be said, is different from our common way of thinking. Our failures we are wont to charge upon circumstances, our unhappiness upon things outside ourselves. Change the circumstances, set things right; to-morrow will be better ! Perhaps so —

if another thing have been set right first. Is God King? Or, in your inmost heart, is Self enthroned as King and God? To the men of His time Jesus found it needful to say, *Repent;* a change of temper, a different attitude, a new outlook, was the most immediate want. Is it otherwise to-day? Are men and women to-day of right temper, is their attitude right, their outlook right? How great the change which most will have to undergo before we can answer in the affirmative! Who will dare say it of himself?

Here, then, Jesus probes and touches to the quick the centre of all human infirmity, misery, and failure; if this can be healed, all can be healed. If men can be brought to a different mind, if they can be persuaded to dethrone self, and to bring all they are and all they have into glad subjection to Him who is Righteousness and Truth and Love, and who desires only to order all lives and all things in accord with His Blessed Character and for their own true good, — then is the better future indeed at hand, already begun. In due time every interest of life shall be lifted up, and all shall be gladdened and strengthened by the health giving Spirit of our King.

II.

The Kingdom of God Within Us.

And being asked by the Pharisees, when the kingdom of God cometh, He answered them and said, The kingdom of God cometh not with observation: neither shall they say, Lo, here! or, There! for lo, the kingdom of God is within[1] you.— LUKE xvii. 20, 21.

[1] Or, *in the midst of you*. — Marginal note, REVISED VERSION.

II.

THE KINGDOM OF GOD WITHIN US.

IT is a question not settled — one which perhaps never can be settled — whether the words of Jesus signify that the kingdom is *within men,* in their inner, hidden lives, or that it is *among His contemporaries,* "among you, even here to-day, if ye Pharisees could but see it." It might seem that if the latter were the true interpretation, we should quite lose our text, and in any case that our text is much weakened by the possible alternative. In reality it is, after all, but a small matter. Jesus discredits all the pomps and artificialities of outward circumstance. The kingdom, He would say, is not coming by armed revolution, by rehabilitation of ancient thrones and reinstatement of dynasties, nor by charters, constitutions, or outward schemes at all. Not with observation — with show; not to be pointed at as conspicuously here, or there: unobtrusive, it shall be present where popular opinion is not chiefly intent on finding it. For men, as we have said, are always looking for the good time to come from new arrangements or new schemes, — political, industrial, social, religious; the real good they overlook, the real principle of regeneration they pass by. This, we take it, — whatever a preposition in the text may mean, — this is the real significance of Jesus' words.

How true, then, those words, in the light of what we have already urged. The Pharisee forgot that where God has His way, and there alone, is God's kingdom. Wherever men respect and cherish what is dear to God, wherever there is a genuine striving after righteousness and truth and love, there the kingdom of God has come, and is coming, and shall come in ever increasing splendor and power. Nicodemus needed, as all men need, to be born anew, to be born from above; for without that he could not see the kingdom of God. Once for all, an enthusiasm cannot be compelled from without; and to follow after righteousness and truth and love with the entire concentration of one's being, — this is nothing less than to be on fire with a new enthusiasm. You can by outward force make a man submit to law, or pay a tax; but by outward force you cannot make him love the law, nor convert the tax into an offering of his soul's affection. God's kingdom — that is, His dominion — is so fine a thing, so inward, so delicate, so absolute, that it cannot be ushered in by the clumsy measures of human device. You may make men desist from wrong-doing, — pains and penalties or arguments of expediency may reach so far; but that is not to make them love and strive after righteousness. You may contrive plans for the dissemination of knowledge, and bring various forms of pressure to bear on men to avail themselves of opportunities to get information and education and learning; but that will be powerless to effect a genuine love for truth. You may legislate and organize and reconstruct for the purpose of bettering industrial and social conditions, you may compel men to some sort of justice in dealing with their fellows, and it will be very good so far as it goes; but you cannot compel them from their hearts to honor all men, and love their neighbor as themselves. There is, no doubt, very much of all these things which can be done, and should be done, and which is excellent in its place ; but put it all together, and it will produce but a negative sort of righteousness and truth and love. The kingdom of God, however, means the absolute enthronement of these in the soul of man; man shall bow down to them and embrace them with his whole heart; though there were no external constraint, though there were no penalty affixed, man must still do them because he himself freely chose them: this is the true kingdom of God over man, — none other is; and this is, as we say, a matter of *kingdom within.*

Are not such all true supremacies which result in best service — *kingdoms within?* Are not all the highest callings of men such as demand this sort of inner devotion, — we might almost say passion, — if they are to be followed to any purpose? The crowning achievements of the centuries, — which are held in immortal honor because they bear witness to the true glory of the race, — was it the fear of penalty or the hope of reward from which they sprang? Indeed, are not the best things in every human life, — the things which, it may be at very rare intervals, show the true grandeur and the innate nobility of the man or the woman, — are they not such as come by an inner impulse, with a spontaneousness never seen in the ordinary mechanical routine and spiritless drudgery? Shall we expect the life and activities of a kingdom of God, if such there be, to fall below these in essential character? Will God offer affront to the children of men capable of things so large and high, by exacting unwilling tribute from them, or accepting mere formal or grudging service? No; He will take royal homage from you in the way most honorable to Himself and you, as men yield freely of their best at the call of patriotism or of humanity, or to the lifelong service of the art they love, — so, or not at all.

"My meat and drink is to do the will of Him

that sent me." He that uttered these words is the same that heralded the kingdom of God; He proclaimed it as now at hand, — at hand by reason of His coming. Where, then, — in His Messiahship; in His Church; in His Heaven, promised to the believing?

Primarily, in none of these; it is *in Himself*. It is, so simple is this truth, in His own perfect, God-devoted human life; in His free, spontaneous obedience, in His lifelong, unwavering devotion to the Father's work, than which He had no other business on earth. The kingdom of God was verily *within Him;* and there it was perfect.

To eyes that can see, there is no more impressive spectacle than such a kingdom. It is not a trick of rhetoric when we say that the empires of earth dwindle in the comparison. It is true, in that "circle of lands" which had then been bound in a peace imposed by a resistless conquest, there was much to dazzle the imagination. The whole known world parcelled out in provinces, governed by the representatives of central Rome, covered with a network of those marvellous roads, watched by sleepless legionaries, — it was in its day a wonderful, and apparently indestructible, system. Yet how hollow in the hour of its seemingly absolute triumph! how speedy its helpless overthrow! In the great Day of the Eternal, which is as a thousand years, what a mushroom growth such an earthly empire! How unsubstantial as a dream, how weak the bond, how ineffectual the rule, which attempted to hold together this mass, and presumed to make it a kingdom! Such is your *kingdom without*, — your world-empire.

Contrast another with it, — one contemporaneous with Rome at her greatest. The humble young Artisan of Palestine proclaims the kingdom of God, which, as we have been saying, He carries about with Him in His own person. There is nothing fanciful in our claim that, confined as yet to Himself, it is already greater than the realm of the Cæsars. One Man against the world! And history gives us the record that there was more power in the one Man than in that world-kingdom, — more conquering, subduing, moulding, reconstructing, organizing, dominating power. There is no denying the fact that He proved mightier.

Nor are we even astonished that it should be so. Given a principle that can so master such a life as His, and what limit will you set to its conquests? For it can command that vast and rarely seen reserve of power in man which, seriously enlisted and marshalled on behalf of what man can thoroughly believe in, honor, and trust, becomes simply invincible. It is a reserve power which ambition and fear, greed and hatred, are alike unable to summon. It will respond to no call but that of righteousness and truth and love.

We are, however, continually miscalculating the strength of the combatants in the unceasing warfare. It is true, numbers are against us. But numbers were against the Greeks at Marathon. We forget that "the very stars in their courses fought against Sisera." We forget that a force is not measured by the actual present area in which we may see it operative, but rather by the intensity and unspent fulness which is the potency of things yet unseen and yet undreamed of. We see that in the triumph of Jesus Christ and the kingdom of God over the empire of the robbers of the ancient world.

There is no question before Christendom to-day which can for a moment compare in importance with this: How may we get men at the present possessed of the power of Jesus, — the secret and method of Jesus, if you prefer to call it that? How may we have among us here and now the potency of such conquest, and the working of such a force? How may we get hold of the unreached, untouched possibilities of character and achievement lying buried under the shallower occupations and interests of gain and pleasure? How may we touch this humdrum mediocrity, and get heroes? How may we clearly discern and practically apply the great principle of spiritual values, making one man worth ten thousand of such as his former self? This is the key to the great problem, for the most part so pettily handled by the present Church of Christ.

The answer is in your Testament. There is none to teach us here but He who alone of men possessed in perfection the thing which we desire. What Jesus said, what He did, what He instructed His chosen representatives to say and do, how they carried out their instructions,— it is all written in those Gospels and Epistles.

Of which the root is, as we must say again, *the kingdom within;* which cannot find a place till there be a resolute renunciation of old ideals, abandonment of old habits of thought, giving way to a different temper, a changed attitude, a new outlook — in a word, *repentance.*

And how does the Master set to work to bring men to this?

He gathers disciples about Him. He bids them do as He does, walk in His footsteps, take His yoke upon them to be guided of Him, keep His commandments. He holds them close to Him; in the intimacy of daily contact they catch His influence, they begin to see things in His light. They experience in due time the bursting of the old barriers of timidity and unbelief and concern for self and regard for the world, and feel the inflowing of His very Life into their lives, in the great Gift of Pentecost. Now they are men of Divine power, and victory attends them.

This was His way with the Twelve. It is essentially still His way with all who would be His disciples. They must leave all and come to Him; they must yield implicit obedience to His directions; they must abide with Him, and open their whole souls to the illumination and quickenning of His Spirit. In all the ages the men of lasting beneficent power have come to it in substantially this way. There had to be a complete breaking with all that would hold back and fetter, a complete self-committal to the Highest the soul could see, an absolute concentration of inmost powers toward the realization of the great Purpose.

The faithful declaration of these conditions has ever been honored of God. The ages of the Church's power, beginning with the Apostolic, have been those in which men took Jesus most seriously, and understood Him to mean what He said, — when He exhorted men to "seek the kingdom first," took Him to mean *first;* when He warned them that "they could not serve God and Mammon," resolved they would have done with Mammon; when He bade them "give up all and follow Him," brought everything and laid it at His feet, for His own disposal of it all. For when men have taken Jesus seriously, they have been able to enter into His thoughts and plans not only concerning themselves, but concerning society, humanity, the world at large with all its complex interests; they have been able to work with Him in those spheres, and to leave upon their generation and their age the mark of that which had transformed themselves. A characterless, compromise Christianity, no matter how numerically large, can never do that. The world needs what is first of all,— a *kingdom of God within us.*

How often has the Church forgotten this! How often has she preferred a kingdom coming with observation! It has always been, it is to-day, her fatal mistake. She began early to sacrifice the pure enthusiasm of apostolic days to greed for power and ambition for self-aggrandizement; she received her reward in the triumphs of earthly empire, of outward pomp, by which the spirit is not satisfied and humanity not blest. She sowed to the flesh, and of the flesh reaped corruption. Bernard of Cluny, in the days of hierarchical glory, sighs and sings of a Heavenly Jerusalem the Golden, transferring the aspirations of a believing soul from a kingdom here to a kingdom hereafter. Is it not a significant thing that so much of our popular Protestantism to-day does the same?

III.

The Kingdom of God coming on Earth.

Thy kingdom come. Thy will be done in earth as it is in heaven. — MATT. vi. 10.

III.

THE KINGDOM OF GOD COMING ON EARTH.

TWO things there are to which the Christian's faith bids him look forward, — the kingdom here, and the kingdom hereafter. And as we were saying, the fundamental mistake of the Church, committed so early and committed so often since, has always tended to hide the nearer of the two from view, and to hold up the remoter with unwearying persistence. This has been just as true of popular Protestantism as of Roman Catholicism.

It is well, therefore, that the Lord's Prayer should bear its daily witness — albeit to dull ears and dull hearts — of just that which we are always forgetting. The petitions taught us by the Master should make it clear that the future world, which we commonly call "heaven," is not more important in God's scheme than the future of humanity in this world, that coming kingdom in which the Divine will shall be done on earth as it is in heaven. Dr. Munger goes still further when he tells us, "The two are to be regarded as one. Regenerated humanity and heaven are interchangeable terms; they are alike, and one simply passes on and up into the other."

We have dwelt at sufficient length upon these two truths, that the kingdom begins in Christ, and that it is always primarily within. It is time now to assert that, being fundamentally of this nature, it must become outwardly manifest, it must be externally embodied; in a word, *it must come on earth*. If there be any belief or sentiment, any emotion or experience, which permanently remains within, and fails to find outward embodiment, and to transform its surroundings — whatever else it may be, it is not that life of God in the soul which is the effect of the Gospel of Christ, *the kingdom within*. A "kingdom within" which does not issue in a "kingdom coming on earth" is but, as Frederic Harrison characterized the abstractions of Herbert Spencer, "the ghost of religion."

"Do we mean there must be a Church?" While we mean much more, we do certainly mean that. Without it the Christian's Creed is incomplete. Because we believe in a God revealed to us in Father, Son, and Holy Ghost, we also, by necessity, believe in a Holy Catholic Church, the Communion of Saints. From all who make the Church "an afterthought;" from all who regard her as a merely human institution, organized at the volition of men, therefore to be abandoned at will, and supplanted by another; from all who would reduce her to the level of a club, exercising their choice as to inclusion and exclusion by man-made tests and standards; and from all who hold the Christian life to be an individual concern, equally possible apart from her communion, — let us testify our everlasting dissent. How can we confess a Father, and yet deny His household? How confess a Son, our Lord, and yet deny His brotherhood, the faithful company of His servants? How confess a Holy Spirit, and yet deny His habitation in the temple of Christian communion? The Church is essential, in the sense that we cannot conceive of the Gospel finding lodgment in human society without the direct manifestation of its presence and power in a fellowship, sacred, united, continuous. Of the spiritual kingdom of God, the Church is the necessary embodiment.

We shall doubtless be met with the objection that the Church of history is disfigured with wrongs, falsehoods, and hatreds which are the exact opposite of the righteousness and truth and love of the kingdom of God. Let us make no effort to conceal or to minimize these deplorable faults. But let us also remember that if a man may be a holy man without being absolutely free from error and sin, so also may the Church be holy without being infallible. Moreover, it must not be forgotten that the crimes committed in the name of the Church were mostly committed by those who had gained power within her and exercised an unprincipled "ring" rule over her, silencing all protests and crushing out all opposition — in reality her enemies and not her representatives; as, indeed, personal and political reasons have moved to probably the larger part of the cruelties and tyrannies practised against nonconformists in all ages. In the face of it all we will dare assert that in every age the reign of righteousness and truth and love has been very decidedly *within* the bounds of the Church, rather than *without*. When we say "the Church," we do not mean, of course, the hierarchy, or the clergy, or the accredited spokesmen, but the Society in its entirety; out of whose obscurer membership has ofttimes come the prophet of a new age, with rebuke and promise. As, indeed, her worship and her ordinances, nay, her very presence, stood among men a continuous, living witness of the claims of righteousness, and truth, and love.

That the witness has not been ineffectual; that, in other words, the kingdom of God embodied in the Church extended its sway to realms lying beyond its immediate boundary lines, exerting its influence upon human society as such, — this also we may read in history. Taking, for instance, the peoples of Europe, among whom the Church was established, can anything be plainer than the constant moral progress from Saint Paul's day to our own? In civil government, in social customs, in business, everywhere outside the distinctively "religious" life as well as within it, there has been a change for the better. To argue the point would be a waste of time. Difference of opinion as to the fact itself, there is none; the disagreement arises only when we assign its cause.

For there are still multitudes of people, some thoughtful and well informed, others taken captive by a sounding word, who will explain all this as "an evolution." To whom we make reply that we have no objection to their calling it what they please, only so they do not leave us to the folly of believing that *the earth makes itself better.* *The earth never makes itself better:* you may set that down at once for a settled fact!

John Fiske, in that brilliant lecture of his on "Manifest Destiny," sketches the future of civilization in its progress from the horrors of warfare to the blessedness of universal peace. The development of industrialism and the inevitable pressure of competition are to terminate at length this cruel, monstrous, wasteful mode of settling international disputes. The argument is admirable, but somehow one can hardly help feeling that the most important matter has been left untouched. "Competition," "industrialism," these are not words so ill-favored as "war" and "aggrandizement;" but, in this Dictionary of the age to come, will they not trace down to the same roots, of *self* and *greed?* Unrestrained by ethical motives, the selfishness which curses individuals and societies will break out in open violence, to carry its point, if open violence serve its purpose best; if by some other method its end will be more effectually reached, some other method it will employ. There is, therefore, in the end no sufficient force to deter from war save the infusion of the essential spirit of what we have called the Kingdom of God. Leave that out, circumstances may arise in which it may seem that a war of aggression promising great material advantage can be waged with impunity, and what will prevent the wrong? Woe to the people with whom no consideration higher than that of advantage shall intervene both to direct and to restrain!

But suppose that wars should cease by reason of the unprofitableness of blood-shedding. Perhaps it is not so brutal a sentiment as at first it appears when Von Moltke says, " Without war the world would stagnate, and lose itself in materialism." God forbid that it should be necessary to continue the slaughter of our fellow-men in order to hold materialism in check! What we know is that "industrialism" ("business" some prefer to call it) in time of peace perpetrates by "competition" horrors as terrible as those of war. Charles Kingsley, in his "Cheap Clothes and Nasty," pictured them in grim language; and the worst of it was that the greater part of the tract consisted simply of figures and statements of fact quoted from the poor victims themselves. None too strongly did he say, " Folks are getting somewhat tired of the old rodomontade that a slave is free the moment he sets foot on British soil! Stuff! — are these tailors free? Put any conceivable sense you will on the word, and then say — are they free?" And again, "Sweet competition! Heavenly maid! — Now a days hymned alike by penny-a-liners and philosophers as the ground of all society — the only real preserver of the earth! . . . 'These are thy works, thou parent of all good!' Man eating man, eaten by man, in every variety of degree and method!"

It will not do to say, that was in England, a generation ago! How many years is it since a Parliamentary commission investigated the sweating system, and brought its undiminished abominations officially to light? — In England? What, then, has Helen Campbell to say about our own land? And Jacob A. Riis? Of the mass of fiction dealing with these things we say not a word. Statistics and instantaneous photographs furnish us enough food for sober reflection. It does seem as if, when left to itself, the world out of every new discovery and invention forged the implements of a new tyranny, to crush out the hopes of the weak, to set up some new bondage in the place of one just overthrown, and in short-sighted, greedy wickedness to destroy the greatest of all values, — humanity and human life.

And when we cry out against such a state of things as Charles Kingsley and Helen Campbell have denounced, we are told, "It cannot be helped. Business is business." Precisely so; this is our very contention. It is only when you call in what is not business, what is of quite a different and higher order, that you get any help. If might makes right, and self-interest is supreme, it is a waste of breath to appeal to men to refrain from oppression and extortion. "Business is business!"

Prof. Joseph Le Conte is a good enough evolutionist, we think, to satisfy any reasonable requirement. It might be well for all those who, speaking much of "Evolution," really seem to mean thereby that the world is indebted to itself for its improvement, to read what he has to say of the indispensableness of the Christ in the process of the development of the race.[2] "The Christ," he writes, "must reveal the right way of life before we can follow, and transform our characters thereby. . . . This Divine ideal can never again be lost, because it is itself the agent of its own realization."

Saint John, in his Apocalyptic vision, "saw the holy city, new Jerusalem, coming down out of heaven from God." This has not yet ceased to be a fitting figure of the earth's redemption and the true progress of humanity, — a figure not primarily, as we take it, of the blessed life after death, but of the kingdom of God coming on earth. The secret of its presence, which at the same time is the pledge of its final triumph, is that essentially it is come down out of heaven from God.

True, its progress must be slow. It is a vast mass which is to be lifted and held up. The amount of change to be wrought is tremendous, and the opposing factors are great and strong. Again and again it has seemed as if the kingdom had come with observation, — as if one might say of it, "Lo, here!" or, "There!" — and men have thought that now at length, by one great bound, the reign of righteousness and truth and love on earth had been fully ushered in. Exceptional

[1] Andover Review, July, 1891. "The Relation of the Church to Modern Scientific Thought."

circumstances, not to be maintained for any length of time, have made experiments possible whose brief success has been less instructive than their ultimate failure. Savonarola's Florence and Calvin's Geneva do not endure.

In all this there is no cause for discouragement. John Henry Newman, in one of his exquisite little hymns, utters the prayer which we all have need to pray, —

> "Lord! who Thy thousand years dost wait
> To work the thousandth part
> Of Thy vast plan, for us create
> With zeal a patient heart."

Meanwhile can we not see how, in God's vast plan, the kingdom is to take outward possession of this poor sin-burdened earth? Through the succession of God-inspired men full of holy enthusiasm the impulse is imparted to well-meaning but shorter-sighted bodies of men, and so the movement is communicated, still from God, through His prophets to the people. And as of old time, though with the freedom which belongs to the Spirit, the prophets of the preparation came from His chosen Israel, so still to-day, with the same freedom, the prophets of the coming kingdom arise (albeit not necessarily from the priestly lines or the straitest sect) within the borders of His Church. At the present hour it is precisely one of the most cheering of all signs that in the Church at large more heed is paid to Saint Paul's great exhortation, "Quench not the Spirit; despise not prophesyings; prove all things; hold fast that which is good." A freer and a purer Church, nursing mother of great witnesses and of leaders filled with holy enthusiasm, furnishing moreover not only leaders, but increasingly also large and earnest bodies of followers in the great campaign, — next to our faith in the Triune God of our redemption is our faith in her, the pillar and ground of the truth!

"I love Thy kingdom, Lord,
The house of Thine abode,
The Church our blest Redeemer sav'd
With His own precious blood!

"Sure as Thy truth shall last,
To Zion shall be given
The brightest glories earth can yield,
And brighter bliss of heaven."

IV.

The Universal Kingdom of God.

"Thou didst put all things in subjection under his feet." For in that He subjected all things unto Him, He left nothing that is not subject unto Him. But now we see not yet all things subject unto Him. — HEB. ii. 8.

IV.

THE UNIVERSAL KINGDOM OF GOD.

THERE is a peculiar turn of thought in this writer's use of the Psalm quotation: referring primarily to man, as the crown of creation, it is here applied to Jesus, in a manner at first sight difficult to understand. A key to it, perhaps, is in the fact that the whole significance of Jesus, when spoken of in connection with the world-order, is in His perfect humanity. Surely if the ideal man, the man as his Creator designs him, is "crowned with glory and honor," is "set over the works of His hands," and may be said to have "all things put in subjection under his feet"—*then Jesus;* for Jesus *is* what man is designed and created to be.

Those who have followed us in the observations thus far made respecting the principles of the kingdom of God, may reasonably ask, "Do you honestly expect that the theory you have set forth will ever find complete practical embodiment? What you have said about the Divine will and government, and the true laws of human welfare and progress, is all well enough: but do you really think that the earth will ever see such a state of things as you depict? Do you sincerely look for a time when the domain of the Christian Gospel and of Christian Society will be more than provincial, — will become what may fairly be called *Universal?*"

The question is a fair one, and the text we think covers it fairly on both sides. "He left nothing that is not subject unto Him. But now we see not yet all things subject unto Him." We are quite ready to give the categorical answer, *Yes.* We do look for the kingdom of God to be yet, in due time, universal.

We admit that we see not yet all things subject unto Him, — vast areas of humanity still unsubdued, still unreached, unclaimed.

We look at the actual present population of the globe, and see the millions on millions of our race who are not yet so much as touched by the first ray of the Gospel. Several years ago an eminent English churchman, Canon Taylor, stirred the religious public by an article on "The Great Missionary Failure." The startling picture of the non-Christian populations of Asia and Africa increasing annually at the rate of more than eleven millions, with an annual increase of native Christians of only some sixty thousand; to say nothing of his description of the aggressiveness and strength of Mohammedanism, — we do not regret his forcing them upon the Christian world, for it is our business to deal with facts and to take all the facts into account. We would not forget, moreover, the vices and wrongs of which Europeans and Americans on missionary soil are so often guilty; the intemperance, immorality, greed, and fraud, exhibited by those who have come from Christian lands and are taken as representatives of the Christian religion. Rum in Africa, opium in Asia, avarice in both, these are worse things for the missionary to contend against than superstition, ignorance, and unbelief; bad enough in themselves, but in this connection a hundredfold worse because they are the shame of *his* people.

Turn from lands we call "heathen" to those we call "Christian." What is the ethical and spiritual condition of the nations of Europe, for example? Great Britain, Germany, France, Russia, — call the roll down to the smallest; is the kingdom of God conspicuously dominant in any of them? See their huge standing armies, the combustible material for a conflagration of war more terrible in its magnitude than perhaps any in history. Mark their statesmanship, and note the principles which appear to govern their dealings with one another. Look into their inner life; observe the different classes of society among them; are righteousness and truth and love enthroned there? Go through their great cities; see the luxury on the one hand, the pauperism on the other: let one who knows tell you of the corruption existing unrebuked, unpunished, the intrenched immorality which is a constant threat to the law-abiding people of the community. And how much better is our own nation, which is pleased to regard itself as pre-eminently in the favor of the Almighty and quite indispensable to His plans? America, with the haste of its people to get rich, and the bitterness of large classes who find themselves outstripped in the race; with a "sweating" system of our own; with private wars waged between the hired soldiery of great corporations and their dissatisfied employees; with the shame of our treatment of the Indian and other inferior races, when here and there they seem to stand in the white man's way; with the saloon, the gambling room, the brothel, flourishing and multiplying, and with the official complicity with vice; with seventy-five per cent. of our young men never entering the church door; with the domination of the dangerous classes in our city politics the land over, and the dictation of terms and candidates by the organized corruption of the community; with the sale, virtually, of positions of high honor and trust in our civil government, — altogether there are many things in our national life "not yet subject unto Him."

Nor, where we look for light, can we candidly say that everything is bright and encouraging. Consider the condition of the Christian Church in her most advanced and "evangelical" branches: how little genuine faith, how much petty timidity, trimming and time-serving; what gingerly handling of the great commandments of Christ; loud professions joined with self-pampering and inability to endure hardness; zeal for orthodoxy and apathy toward the real triumph of our Lord! Is it an ugly statement? Judge for yourselves if it does not exhibit fairly one side of the situation!

No, we do not yet see all things subject unto Him.

Nevertheless they yet shall be. We accept it as a principle of faith. We believe it upon Christ's own word, and upon that of His servants who spake moved by His Spirit. We accept it as a conclusion of reason; for we cannot conceive of the ultimate triumph of evil over good, of falsehood over truth. We accept it as the logical conclusion of what we ourselves have seen and learned of the progress of the Kingdom down to the present.

For, as we have already said, that the world nevertheless is better, and is growing better, admits of no serious denial. Doubtless one reason why we may draw up such a catalogue of "things not yet subject unto Christ" is that we are now in possession of more searching tests, of higher standards. The very conceptions and ideas that now gain acknowledgment, and so enter by education into the moral veins of the rising generation, are better and higher conceptions and ideas than men used to have. When the common thought embraces the recognition of righteousness and truth and love, — and this it is doing in an ever-increasing measure, — it is but the acknowledgment, conscious or unconscious, that it is right that all things should be made subject unto Him. The acknowledgment must thenceforth draw after it the realization of such an order of things, by the compulsion of conscience and common-sense. The fact must, however tardily, follow the idea.

And it is well for us to remember that God is not confined to ways and methods now employed, nor to a rate of progress such as His kingdom now exhibits. The centuries seemed to lie dormant till at the proper hour, in the fulness of time, the fearful abuses of the mediæval Church were assailed and overthrown. And again, save for internal dissensions, the Church seemed to have forgotten to work and fight till the century of foreign missions was ushered in. Church history, and all history, has been full of surprises.

THE UNIVERSAL KINGDOM OF GOD.

Long preparing in secret, the new order has again and again burst forth upon an astonished world. There is nothing magical, nothing arbitrary, in it; the factors were all there, and if one had seen and known them, he could have foretold the inevitable result.

So, if we would look again at the great missionary field of the world, and bring together what there is of past and present achievement, we should find it of actually larger dimensions than the numerical exhibit given us by Canon Taylor. The figures may be correct enough, and the task before the Church is doubtless of gigantic magnitude; and yet the figures do not tell the whole story, nor does magnitude mean hopelessness. It is not so very long since the annual increase of native Christians was by no means sixty thousand. There is no unalterable edict that it shall not exceed that number, or that proportion toward the annual increase in the pagan populations. We cannot forget Japan; and the actual present gain in converts may be small, while yet the advance of the forces of the kingdom of God toward the conquest of the dark places of the earth may be rapid and victorious, — only that the point has not been reached where all that has been gained shall fully appear. Who that is at all familiar with the work of the foreign missionary will need to be told that it often involves years of digging and laying foundations ere the first stone of the visible structure can be laid? But from that very fact the foreign missionary sees in most lands, as the result of his efforts, not only individual lives won for his Lord, and churches organized, but the adoption of better ideas in government, in social life, in business; he sees the outward form, and in a degree the inner spirit, of pagan society considerably affected, sometimes materially changed. If Canon Taylor can justly charge — and probably in the case of some he can — that "European missionaries fail because they attempt to make Asiatics or Africans into middle-class English Philistines," it would still not follow that Christianity will not be ultimately triumphant among all the peoples of the earth, in a form adapted to the national and racial peculiarities of each. Surely there is every reason to believe that so fundamental a principle will obtain general recognition sooner or later, and then we may expect the missionary to succeed as, in some parts, he does not now.

After all, the final question regarding the kingdom among heathen peoples comes to this: Is not the very fact that what the Christian missionary has to bring them is better in itself, and better in its accompanying effects, than what they now possess, — is not this itself the pledge that the most open-minded, the wisest, and the best among them will accept it? If any people have once fairly had the Christ brought to their view, is not their destiny thereafter fixed; are they not bound thenceforth either to accept or to reject Him ; and will not the process begun go on to its completion? Remember the saying of Le Conte, the evolutionist, "This Divine Ideal can never again be lost, because it is itself the agent of its own realization." It may be a thing difficult to conceive that the teeming millions of Asia and Africa are yet to be Christianized, at least as thoroughly as the populations of Europe and America are now ; but to conceive of their being of the same race, the same humanity, with ourselves, and learning of the Christ, as they are fated to learn more and more in this day of ever-extending intercourse, without being profoundly affected, even transformed, — to conceive that, we say, would far more stagger our powers of imagination. No one who has read history to any purpose will seriously question what the outcome must be. The rejection of the Christ by some will no more hinder His acceptance by others, and His virtual enthronement ultimately over all, than the like rejection, accompanied by brutal and fiendish persecutions, did in Jerusalem or in Rome. And whatever new garb of philosophic doctrine, of polity, or of cultus, Christianity may assume among those nations yet to be converted, it will be the reign of our common Lord Jesus Christ, the same yesterday, to-day, and forever.

Look once more also at the Christian world, so-called. There, we have already said in no ambiguous way, we do not yet see all things subject unto Him. May we also see any indications of their coming subjection? May we see any signs of the progress of the kingdom in Christendom itself? What hopes have we, on what are they centred?

We have spoken of the higher conceptions and the loftier standards now held up before us as an evidence of progress, even while they may serve to discourage us in the judgments they compel us to pronounce upon our times. If we were asked to state in what particulars we have reached a higher conception of Christianity, we should answer: In two. In the first place, we are increasingly coming to regard Christianity as more than a religion, — a life. Religion addresses man on one side of his nature; the Gospel addresses itself to the *whole man,* and claims him entirely. With that change of view ensues, not a secularization of things heretofore held sacred, but a sanctification of things heretofore held common, — with possibly less emphasis upon things peculiarly "sacred." In the second place, Christianity is no longer left to begin and end in the individual's rescue from perdition, but is held to be equally a social matter, — indeed, not itself until it does become a social matter, — so that fellowship, brotherliness, co-operation for all worthy ends, from lowliest to highest, in a word, *love*, is taken to be its crowning manifestation.

It is possible, of course, to press these views too far, — not, indeed that they could be too strongly stated, but that they might be urged to the exclusion of other truths no less indispensable. But holding them in their proper relation, and, if you will, with utmost intensity, they are a substantial gain to our own spiritual possessions, and a mighty help to the coming of the kingdom of God.

For it is precisely along these two lines of thought that men generally are to-day open to appeal. Take the popular addresses of Professor Drummond, for example, and observe how he presses home again and again these views of Christianity and of the Christian life, and how his booklets are seized with avidity by the public, like bread by the starving. And have not people been starving, lo! these many years? — starving for the Gospel of Jesus Christ in its simplicity and yet comprehensiveness. Candidly, has the preaching of the Christian ministry as a whole supplied what humanity has most needed?

Indeed we may note the beginnings of a decided change in the pulpit of to-day. The message is becoming direct, living, practical, in the best sense of those hackneyed adjectives. Evangelistic addresses, so long marked as a whole by unreality and remoteness, which was poorly covered by lurid rhetoric and heated emotion, — evangelistic addresses are partaking of the new spirit, and are in consequence taking hold by their true ethical and spiritual power of the busy populations of our great cities. Other signs of the change are beginning to appear on every hand.

A great German theologian, Rothe, carries out his philosophy to the conclusion that ultimately the Christian State will supplant the Christian Church. His thought was that while the Church as commonly conceived is but partial, the Christian State would be universal; whereas in the former some worship, in the latter all would both live and worship to the glory of God and in the name of Christ. Industry, statesmanship, art, literature, science, — all would be dedicated to God, all would be at the service of humanity.

The dream is a splendid one; whether in such a form it shall ever come to pass need not concern us; neither need we be concerned regarding those other questions of speculative interest which even our Lord encountered when one asked Him, "Lord, are they few that be saved?" and he made reply, "Strive to enter in by the narrow door." Enough for us to know that His kingdom cannot suffer defeat or check; that all its triumphs mean increase of blessing to men, because its triumphs are the triumphs of righteousness and truth and love; that to us is given the unspeakable privilege of fighting under Him and laboring with Him whom God hath highly exalted, and given the Name which is above every name; "that in the Name of Jesus every knee should bow, of things in heaven, and things on earth, and things under the earth; and that every tongue should confess that Jesus Christ is Lord, to the glory of God the Father."

V.

Great Joy to All People.

Behold, I bring you good tidings of great joy which shall be to all the people. — LUKE ii. 10.

V.

GREAT JOY TO ALL PEOPLE.

"JOY." What joy? If it be only such as this world often brings, heralded with much flourish, keenly anticipated — the longer we live, the less shall we be thrilled by the announcement. For the greater part of these joys are very meagre joys, long in coming, quickly gone. Is there anything, then, in what this angel says? — anything for men and women to whom disappointment and sorrow have often come; who have perhaps begun to think that the momentary lull of quiet but forebodes another storm? — or for those whose very abundance of prosperity has given them a surfeit of pleasures, and who have grown sceptical of the existence of any satisfying and enduring joy? Oh, Angel of Bethlehem, to how many incredulous ears and weary hearts is thy message repeated this day!

"Great joy?" How often are the children of men deceived in their expectations of a great joy. The acquisition of what is strangely called a "fortune," meaning large possessions, does experience prove that a great joy? Even if it were not accompanied, as it always is, by added cares and new anxieties, would it be a thing in which the heart of man could for long rest and be satisfied? Has it been, with those who have made the trial? Let us not be cynical in our judgment. Wealth to some has brought much relief, comfort, opportunity for richer and nobler life, as it always ought to do; but has it been a great joy? — that sort of joy with which one may rise in the morning, look it calmly in the face, and say of it, " It is enough; I am content "? — that sort of joy which can circumfuse all things and all happenings with a golden atmosphere, and leave no room in us for secret misgiving and dread of possible calamity and failure? The coming of a fortune to you might mean the ability to do for family and friends the things which you have so often wished for them, to cheer and help, possibly give new lease of life to some dear one; but even so, would it be, could it be, the great good for which your soul is hungering?

How is it with the attainment of fame? Is that the great joy of human life? Grant that it were pure and honestly gotten fame, which so much of the world's fame is not; grant that your fellow-men were judges of it, which they rarely are; grant that, genuine and rightly appreciated, it would remain undimmed and unforgotten for even one brief year, which it will not;

grant that when attained in one form or degree it did not create, as it almost always does, an unnatural thirst for ever more and more, ending how often in morbid egotism, in greediness for praise and adulation, asking for ceaseless incense to the idol, self, — I say, grant that fame were genuine, and appreciated, and kept fresh in this hurrying world, and left you still unspoiled (an accumulation of improbabilities), would it be, even so, the great joy to you? I believe those who have tried would honestly say, and not hesitate a moment to say, "It would not. It could not."

But there are other gifts which are not like these, only for the few; better precisely because they are more common. There is — homely thing to speak of here, but so much lamented when lost — there is health. And that is a joy. Let us not undervalue it. Let us remember that God bestowed His special thought and care on the fashioning of these bodies, on the harmony of their functions and powers, so that when cared for as befits His crowning handiwork, they should praise Him in health, the temples of His Spirit. Strange it is, therefore, but we know that it is true, that some of the healthiest people in the world are not happy. They go when and where others dare not, their bodies do them service as those of their less fortunate fellows cannot; they have vigor, superabounding animal spirits, but no steady radiant joy. You may say they are the exceptions. Perhaps not! But grant it. Suppose men have that perfection of physical equipoise which means bodily comfortableness, and which is, so far as it goes, just what God wishes us to have, does it go far enough to be in itself "great joy"? Great joy for a human being, higher than mere animal organism made for digestion, exercise, and sound sleep? Do there not come into such lives of thoughtless, good-natured health glimpses of deeper things which disturb the evenness of their satisfaction? Thank God! yes. How well-fed comfortableness will avoid where it can the vision of misery and hunger and disease, — vision never cheerful, not pleasing to God Himself, but exhibiting what comes of error, wrong, and sin, and therefore essentially kin to well-fed comfortableness as to shivering poverty. "Thou art the man," spoken to David in his strength and luxury, swept his joys away in an instant. Does not the selfish indifference to others which so often marks those who carefully guard their comfort, shrink from the sight of pain because it fears that at that sight its hideous self will be unmasked? No; let us not be deceived. Health let us seek, let us guard (but not at too great cost to others!), let us thank God for; but let us not say, as we have often heard men say, "So long as I have my health and sufficient income, I want nothing more!"

There are joys, however, which may be still more truly joys, — joys of friendship and of closer affection, in which we begin to feel how far above these lower things our true life rises; and among such, suggested especially by this gladdest of birthdays, is one which may indeed be called a great joy. It is the joy that came to Zacharias and Elizabeth; it is the joy that comes over and over again when a little child claims a place among us and makes home twice home by his blessed advent; when a little life is begun in the midst of us, wonder and mystery ever fresh, promise and possibility of what glorious things to come! The joy which parents have in watching over, guiding, and training their child, even though it cost them toil and suffering, is one of life's greatest joys. But oh, the pangs of disappointment, the agonies of sorrow, when all that love seems wasted; when the child is worse than dead, gone to uselessness, to shame and moral ruin, gone beyond their recall! Where *then* is the joy?

Enough. If there is such a thing as a great joy in which we may infallibly trust, let us know it, and understand clearly what it is and how we may have part in it. Is there, again we ask, such a thing as a joy that will not fail us when we want it most; that will bear transportation from the regions of youth to those of old age, health to infirmity, wealth to want, and through all the sundry chances and changes of this mortal life, will remain steadfast and sure?

The Angel of Bethlehem tells us there is. Again on Christmas-Day his message comes to us, "good tidings of great joy which shall be to all the people." Good tidings, indeed, if the word be not merely a rhetorical figure, but the literal truth: "great joy to all people." This is what we need; this is what a heaven-sent gift should be — to all people! No matter who they may be, high or lowly, — and, indeed, to the lowly came the message first of all, — no matter what sort of house they live in, or what clothes they wear, or whether they have of this world's goods laid by in store; no matter whether cultivated or plain, learned or ignorant; no matter what may have happened to them this twelve-month, or what may be staring them in the face this very day; whether they be young or old, well or ill, beloved in this world or friendless, — a joy to fit them all!

That is too much to promise? Not if there be a Gospel of God at all. If it reach not so far as this, then we have no further business here. Vacate the pulpit, empty the pews, close the church; and when you reach home take your

Bible from its place of honor and of readiest use and put it away upon the shelf beside the Arabian Nights. This is a real world; and if the thing break down in actual life, it were both foolish and wicked to maintain the show of still believing it!

No; it is not too much for God to promise, or for us to expect. Philip still bids us "come and see." Make trial of it. Put it to the test. Let the appeal be, not to Scripture text, but to the witness of experience, to actual life. And there — shall we fear to claim it? — the announcement has been fully sustained. Through the Child born in that radiant night, there has come a new element into the struggle and toil of our human life; a new power to sustain us, a healing virtue to take the sting out of our failures and pains, a glory to fill common things with new splendors, a vital energy to impart to our very enjoyments a new life and zest and reality. The world-old cry, —

> "'T is life, whereof our nerves are scant,
> Oh, life, not death, for which we pant;
> More life, and fuller, that I want," —

has its answer in Him who was proclaimed on Christmas night as the Great Joy of all people, and who came that they might have life, and might have it more abundantly.

For He brought us first of all a truer manhood. If birthdays are worth celebrating in proportion as the lives they usher in are great and worthy, and their effects still present with us; is not Jesus' supremely the birthday for the whole world's commemoration? He who, by what He Himself was, has given to the very word *Man* a new definition, filling it with new content of meaning, exhibiting its yet undreamed-of capacities, "the Man Christ Jesus," shall we not celebrate Him, shall we not rejoice in Him? He has enriched the whole race, and every human being henceforth born into the world owes Him a debt.

And this we set down as the first element of the Great Joy to All People. For this is indeed fundamental. He gives us to know ourselves. He gives us the light of true life. What can all else avail us, us who are men, if we be not living the true life of men? — since, if that prime essential be wanting, all else can but divert for a time, only to bring us back to the great failure, the great emptiness, the defeat of life! At some time destined to arrive and not to be put off forever, at some time if there be any Purpose or Design in creation at all, we must come to terms with that fundamental necessity of being what we were made to be. In that day, not to be what we were made to be, can have but one logical consequence: it is pictured as "outer darkness" and "weeping and gnashing of teeth." Is it not clear as the sun in the heavens that if we lose manhood we lose all? What shall it profit a man if he gain the whole world and lose his own life![1] The day will come when every pleasure and every joy falsely so-called which helped to bring on that great bankruptcy, shall be remembered with bitterness unutterable; yea, every otherwise legitimate joy, even, that was used to silence the deeper cravings of the spirit, shall also appear but loss.

Hail, then, to Him who points us the way, and lends us His hand, and inspires us to the true life for which we are created! Hail to Him who brings to the world the light and power of true manhood! His very warnings shall make us rejoice, His very rebukes shall make us glad, if all the while we can feel that these are pledges to us that we are on the right way, and have nothing to fear being with Him, and shall be partakers of His own crown of manhood at the last!

Yes, warnings and rebukes there must be. Our idea, the world's idea, is not high enough; to come up only to that is to fall below His. The Master takes us in hand in order that he may bring us up to His idea. His idea of a true man was in some essential respects different from that of Jews and Greeks and Romans, so that the very evidences of the strength of His manhood seemed to them marks of weakness. He was derided;

[1] See Revised Testament.

but He triumphed. The "weakness" which from Him passed over into His followers, who became men after His pattern, proved to be of the quality that makes soldiers, heroes, and martyrs. Still the world is not quite ready to approve of His pattern; still men are not ready to give up and be losers, as they think, and so they become the real losers in the end. For he that has heartily accepted the idea of Jesus, he that will lead a true life in Jesus' light, has the secret of a deeper and more real happiness than the world; for out of forbearance, self-denial, sacrifice, he extracts a finer joy. The supreme human satisfaction is his of growing in stature, — of making real gain by every day that he walks with his Master. The end he cannot foresee; he knows not yet what he shall be; but he knows he shall be like Him! Is not that, stripped of all rhetorical unrealities, soberly viewed, and plainly stated, — is not that Great Joy ? To be sure, there is still some remnant of that conflicting principle in his breast; ofttimes he turns his gaze from the great Star of his highest and his honest purpose to fix it upon some will-o'-the-wisp of worldly allurement, and misses his way, sinking into bogs; then he is miserable as the world is miserable, with show of gayety perhaps, as the world wears its mask of gayety; the honest disciple cannot be content to remain there, and will not, nor will his Master leave him there to perish; he will come back again, and more soberly, more calmly, but with deeper because wholesome satisfaction, he will again walk in the light of his Great Joy.

But Jesus brings us what is the ground of that true manhood, — the Fatherhood of God. He came to declare the Father. He said plainly that the love which His disciples saw shining forth from Him was the love of the Father. He taught them that what He exhibited in His treatment of men and His attitude toward them of affection, of sympathy, of tenderness, of self-offering for help and deliverance, of indignation against falsehood, of wrath against wickedness, making up the spiritual "glory" beheld by His apostles, — what He exhibited thus in the narrow confines of brief, circumscribed earth-life, all this is Godhead, this is the Father. Whatever infinitely more than this He may be, — which poor finite human minds cannot take in, — *other* than this He is not; He is nothing which would contradict or destroy this or make it of none effect. Saint John says plainly God is Love. A preacher of to-day has employed the phrase which incorporates the spirit of Saint John's Gospel, "The Christ-likeness of God."

Consider now how great a Joy is this revelation. It drives to the moles and bats forever those idol-notions of Deity which have so long darkened the skies for us. No more philosophical abstractions which chill and terrify, but a living, feeling, loving, helping Father! No more devices of men, blind leading blind, making Him altogether like themselves in narrow jealousy, and petty insistence upon the claims of royal dignity and exaction of penalties, but a Father loving all men as His children, honored in their filial trustfulness, chastising as Love chastises with the relentlessness only of love for men, and hate of no man.

To know that the Supreme Power of the universe is essentially such, that we live under such a rule, and are amenable to such a Judge, — yea, rather, are welcomed to call on such a Defender, whose tenderness toward us passes the tenderness of earthly parents toward their children, — does it not make life a different thing? Is it not the Great Joy for which we have been waiting and hungering, even while we knew not clearly what we lacked?

Giving ourselves in sincerity and with full purpose of heart to Him as we see Him and may touch Him in our blessed Saviour; heeding His call to become His obedient children, and leaving ourselves to the guidance of His well-beloved Son, our Elder Brother; becoming more and more like Him in our thoughts and our estimates of all things, in our purposes and affections, — can it be otherwise than that the troubles, adversities, hindrances, humiliations, disappointments, of life shall all be transmuted into means of blessing to us, and sooner or later become occasions of joy? Saint Paul spoke as one that knew — of tribulation he had surely had his share — when he said, "And to them that love God all things work together for good;" and again, "In all these things we are more than conquerors through Him that loved us. For I am persuaded that neither death, nor life, nor angels, nor principalities, nor things present, nor things to come, nor powers, nor height, nor depth, nor any other creature, shall be able to separate us from the love of God, which is in Christ Jesus our Lord." Could triumph be completer? Has a higher or more exultant joy ever recorded itself in human words? Yet it is perfectly adapted to be, it is essentially, the Great Joy to All People.

> "Once again, O blessed time,
>   Thankful hearts embrace thee;
> If we lost thy festal chime,
>   What could e'er replace thee?
> Change will darken many a day,
>   Many a bond dissever;
> Many a joy shall pass away,
>   But the Great Joy never!"

VI.

The Human Life Divine.

And the Word became flesh and dwelt among us. — JOHN i. 14.

For verily not of angels doth He take hold, but He taketh hold of the seed of Abraham. — HEB. ii. 16.

VI.

THE HUMAN LIFE DIVINE.

"BECAME flesh" — "dwelt among us" — we are in continual danger of practically forgetting that. Could the apostle have put it in a stronger way? "Flesh!" — our own very humanity. "Among us!" — in the very midst of common, every-day people, — fishermen, mechanics, trades-folk — and not up somewhere in the clouds, or in some remote Elysian clime, from our toils and struggles and dull drudgeries far removed.

In the quaint language of the Epistle to the Hebrews it is the same thought. "Not of angels doth He take hold, but He taketh hold of the seed of Abraham." That is to say, He does not assume the angelic condition, and dwell among cherubim and seraphim; He assumes the condition simply of human kind. In both Scriptures there is an endeavor to bring the plain fact right home to our dull understandings, — the plain fact that this perfectly pure, spotless, exalted, and noble life of Jesus was a *human life*, lived in human society, under human conditions; with the same earthly drawbacks, limitations, and besetments that we ourselves so often feel and deplore.

For various reasons it becomes necessary in our day to reassert the dignity of human life. The microscopic scrutiny of motives and character practised in some of our modern literature has done not a little to lower popular estimates of human worth. The weaknesses of the good, the littlenesses of the great, the meannesses of the benevolent, the worldly shrewdness and the insincerities of the religious, — these are laid bare by the skilful touch of clever writers whose chief ambition it seems to be to dispel our illusions and make us quit our idols. It is all well enough, if only we are not brought gradually to sneer at all *ideals*. We cannot help thinking it would be better to believe our common humanity nobler than it is, than to come to doubt whether humanity could be noble at all!

Then there is that great power, modern Science. So many facts relating to man's intellectual and moral life are now partly accounted for by physical causes, that there is an observable tendency among men toward regarding life as a matter of heredity, diet, hygiene, and outward environment. We thank God for Science: for the discovery of wonder upon wonder in the physical part of us; for all we may learn where-

THE HUMAN LIFE DIVINE. 81

by the body shall more efficiently serve the soul. But let us not be blind to the peril that comes with this increased knowledge, when cultivated in a one-sided manner. Instead of lifting up the life, becoming a new impulse to ennoble it, such a pursuit of Science has often served rather to degrade, to deaden the sense of the spiritual. What a dreary wisdom is this which loves to thrust upon us on every occasion the evidences of our kinship with the brute, and never has the time or the inclination to seek proofs of our kinship with the Divine; and how often it poses (of course, unjustly enough) as the latest Word of Science about us!

To be sure the real trouble is, that in our own daily lives, and their actual experience, there is so much to give comfort to these belittling views. There, if we wished, or even against our wish, we might find much which, coldly scrutinized, will awaken no admiration, hardly even respect. Nay, we may leave out of consideration faults and vices of character altogether; and in the unavoidable transactions of the earthward side of our existence will see what appears to detract from the dignity of human life. When we sit down, under the cloud of some particularly depressing mood, and think it all over, — the lifeless routine, the spiritless drudgeries, the petty economies, the trivial concerns about the outward fashion of our conduct and the comment of our neighbors, the many miserable slaveries to which by our own weakness we submit, as well as the self-denials which, half-heartedly undergone, leave us often more embittered than ennobled; every profession and calling confronted with the vital bread-and-butter question, and every variety of service in Church and Nation turned into a marketable commodity, or a means of gratifying personal ambition, — I say, when in this mood we think it all over, and array all the facts of this baser class as witnesses, surely the verdict is not long delayed, "Human life is not a very noble thing!"

Therefore the more need to reassert its essential dignity. And is it not one aim of the Gospel of the Son of Man to do this very thing?

Who can help seeing that the mere fact of the association of Jesus with our earth-life has unspeakably elevated and ennobled and dignified humanity? As after the visit of a royal personage the table at which he dined, the chair on which he sat, the door at which he entered, the street along which his equipage was drawn, are shown to the admiring gaze of loyal subjects, and henceforth are distinguished and held higher and worthy of remembrance in future years, — so has everything that this King's Son in His earthly sojourn touched become ennobled. And thank

God He has touched everything! He touched infancy: it has been a holier thing by reason of the Christ-child. He touched youth: it became thoughtful as well as hopeful, obedient and serious as well as daring; young manhood, and His unobtrusive industry sanctified the service of waiting till God calls; mature life, and its burdens were lifted out of despondency, its battles offset by an unfailing inward peace, its round of duties transfigured by the thought, "It is My meat and drink to do the will of Him that sent Me." He touched the sorrows and troubles of humanity: the prayer, "Not My will, but Thine, be done," has given them all a new meaning. Death itself He touched, and His assurance, "He that believeth on me, though he die, yet shall he live," followed by His own Calvary and His Easter morning, transformed the indignity of the grave into a triumphal entrance to fuller life. He touched, though not by personal participation, the sins and vices of humanity: sympathy for the transgressor, charity for the erring, an open door of return for the worst prodigal,— this is what has come of His taking hold of fallen man. Think, then, for a moment what the human life would be without these transforming influences that have come into the thought and feeling of men from the visit of the Blessed Lord to these earth-shores, from those touches of ennoblement on every age, condition, and circumstance!

And think again. A royal visitor might thus pass through a province, leaving on every hand tokens of benevolence, of enduring influence for good perhaps; yet as a stranger only he might come, as a stranger sojourn, as a stranger return to his regal home.

Not so with this Son of Man. Let us again be reminded that he identifies Himself completely with us; He becomes a naturalized citizen of our country, sharing what we have, foregoing what we have not; He empties Himself; He takes up the whole great load of the human life, — takes it as He finds, makes no complaint of its hard conditions, but lives under them the True Man.

I do not believe any of us half realize how hard Jesus' life was, — speaking of it simply in the way of daily conduct, doing one by one the things He found Himself called to do as a man determined to live a right life, — simply that, without regard to His unique mission. And it was a grand life He lived; no candid, thoughtful man but will reverently acknowledge it. There was nothing small, nothing perfunctory, nothing mediocre, nothing mercenary, in it or about it; it was a towering mountain-peak of high thinking, feeling, doing, and the more so that it was all without show of being heroic.

Such a life, you and I are wont to think, is possible to the smallest minority only of those most favorably circumstanced, — everything in their culture, their means, their surroundings, their family, their friends, their land, and their times conspiring to bring to flower and fruit the finest possibilities of human life. All untoward elements of birth and education and calling and associations and external influences must be as far as possible eliminated; then you may get a noble and harmonious human life. Perhaps we are not altogether wrong; but let us examine more closely Jesus' case.

If great men are the product of the age in which they appear, then look for no Christ in the age of Tiberius and Herod, — an age when the political fabrics were going to rapid dissolution, and the thought of neither Jew nor Gentile any longer held fast to mighty convictions or lofty ideals. What an atmosphere for a Jesus to breathe!

Nor was there a nation remote from civilized luxury and corruption, stern in primitive integrity, patriotic even if not powerful, out of which He might arise, recognized of them as their choicest representative and their truest son. Alas! Israel, you well know, was not such a nation. An unclean foreigner lording it over their religion; Rome-fawning dandies filling a mock-royal court whose kingship had to be begged from every successive emperor; insurrection and riot in the capital, — uprisings without dignity or character, — there was no national life there that should make it on any account a proud thing for a man to say, "I am a Jew." And when He came, "His own received Him not." There was no nation to help this Jesus to be its hero.

How was it with His family and kin? There was help there, — a godly mother, with her work of early training. There was integrity; there was industry. There were simply those things which would combine to help a boy to become a plain, honest, God-fearing man, — just, by the way, what most people among us would not much covet. He abode in that humble life till He began to teach, being then about thirty years of age. But what concerns us now is this: When Jesus does launch forth upon a larger, higher life, it certainly is not His family and His kin that urge or help Him on. He awakens opposition by His teaching; timidly His mother and brethren press on through the crowd that surrounds Him, hoping to make Him desist. He is gathering disciples; but His own brethren do not believe in Him. For His enthusiasm they have no sympathy; His undertaking is to them probably erratic, perhaps presumptuous; His ideals to them are dreams, — dangerous dreams, illusions.

One more circumstance let us note, for it is deemed an all important one. Jesus enlarged His life, carried it to ever higher planes of usefulness and influence, by no improvement of His worldly condition. Let us state the plain fact: culture, as men called it, Jesus had not. There had been no opportunity for it in His family circumstances. Perfect politeness, — expression of a kind and thoughtful heart; sensitiveness to the proprieties, though far as possible from the petty anxieties of etiquette; keen intelligence, as of thinker, seer, philosopher, but not the learning of the scholar; a store of sacred knowledge out of the Scriptures, but not the book-worm accumulations of the Scribes; a love of beauty fed on familiar sights of grass, and flowers, and birds of the air, the simple poetry of nature and our common life seen in tenderness and sympathy and faith, — such as these constitute a culture that was real, genuine, priceless, but not the kind of culture which "society" in His day or in ours would call by that name. This is the plain fact. And His culture being of this kind, He could be and could remain the true nobleman even while He had not where to lay His head. If it absolutely requires libraries, pictures, works of art, elegance, and civilized refinements to exhibit the highest dignity of human life, — to raise up our existence to a level where it shall command respect, admiration, reverence, — then all we can say to Christians is: the highest, most dignified, Life that our poor earth ever knew was lived without these.

And remember *how!* For it was not in hermit retirement; not in renunciation of these things from sheer disdain of them. He still lived a life among men; and all this which He endured, — the poverty, the comparative friendlessness, the rancor of unjust animosities, — all this did not embitter Him, did not sour His temper, did not cast a gloom on His views of life, did not distort His vision, did not wring from Him one impatient word, one morbid syllable.

One thing is established: this human life *can* be lived in a noble way, and that too in circumstances commonly deemed the most prosaic, disheartening, depressing, embittering. Poverty shall not necessarily prevent it; the loneliness of being misunderstood and hated without cause shall not forbid it; no dulness of the times, of the generation in which we live, of the vocation we are compelled to follow, shall defeat it: *it can be so lived because it has been so lived.* The conditions are not of themselves so degrading as to make it impossible. If you ask, What are the possibilities of human life? I answer in a word,

Jesus Christ. Do I mean of your life, of my own life? The record gives me no choice but to say, Yes. We have no right to seek Jesus' glory by arguing, "What He was no one else can be or can become." He does not choose to be exalted in that way. Far off in our case, because our case is one of desperate moral enfeeblement through sin, far off and yet approaching nearer daily if we are sincere disciples, — is this becoming just like Jesus. That is the definite goal of Christian hope and effort. We must reach it by little steps; but every step counts.

Do not look too far for Christ-like attainments; they are under your very eyes, if you will but look. There is a noble, heavenly dignity in all manner of toil and help: there is dignity in the drudgery; there is dignity in the so-called humble graces; dignity in patience, in the little charities, the caresses that warm and cheer the loved one at your side, the little courtesies, the little acts of self-control, the little unseen tests of bravery oft endured, — more brave than the valor that takes cities by storm. When we learn this lesson, we begin to approach in kind the dignity of Jesus' life. Outward grandeur that had not; it by inward grandeur exalted everything He said and did: no other life has ever so done that; therefore is His the noblest.

How shall we find the power to hold to so

high a resolve? Not in ourselves,—no, God be thanked! we are not expected to find that in ourselves. "He taketh hold" of our lives, if we permit Him, and becomes our Saviour by lifting up and holding up our life where it should be. Nay, it will be *His life in ours,* upon ours, alongside ours; so ever-present that our familiar streets and shops and dwelling-places shall be as much linked with Him as the oft-named places of Judea and Galilee, and everywhere we shall feel the solemnity of hallowed association.

> "This is the earth He walked on; not alone
> That Asian country keeps the sacred stain;
> 'T is not alone the far Judean plain,
> Mountain and river! Lo, the sun that shone
> On Him, shines now on us; when day is gone
> The moon of Galilee comes forth again
> And lights our paths as His. . . .
> The air we breathe He breathed,—the very air
> That took the mould and music of His high
> And godlike speech. Since then shall mortal dare
> With base thought front the ever-sacred sky,
> Soil with foul deed the ground whereon He laid
> In holy death His pale, immortal head?"

Yes, truly ours too is a Holy Land. Our life too should be, is called to be, a Divine life. For this purpose He became flesh and dwelt among us,—to hallow our human life, show its possibilities and its original intent by His own living, and give unto all who will receive Him the power to become sons of God.

" Oh, mean may seem this house of clay,
   Yet 't was the Lord's abode ;
Our feet may mourn this thorny way,
   Yet here Immanuel trode.

" Oh, mighty grace, our life to live,
   To make our earth divine !
Oh, mighty grace Thy heaven to give,
   And lift our life to Thine ! "

VII.

Pure Religion.

Pure religion and undefiled before our God and Father is this, to visit the fatherless and widows in their affliction, and to keep himself unspotted from the world. — JAMES i. 27.

VII.

PURE RELIGION.

A MODERN writer[1] tells the story of two old men, Yefim and Yelisei, neighbors in a Russian village, who resolved to make a pious pilgrimage to Jerusalem. Having arranged their affairs at home, and provided themselves with the necessaries for so long a journey, which was to be accomplished on foot, they turned their faces toward the Holy City. After journeying some weeks they passed through a famine-stricken region, and found the distress greater and greater as they went.

One day as they were going through a large village, Yelisei, weary and faint with thirst, turned into a hut for a drink of water. Now Yefim was stronger than his companion, and not caring to stop he went on, leaving Yelisei to overtake him. We may remark, by the way, that Yefim was one of those men whose habits are correct, but whose nature has become self-centred and rather cold and devoid of sympathy and tenderness, — a good man, doubtless, but

[1] Count Tolstoi.

one whose goodness was rather chilling and discouraging; while Yelisei was perhaps lacking in what his neighbor would term "strength of character;" but in all his dealings loved his neighbor as himself, had a childlike trust and affection toward his Father in heaven, and was always open to any call for help and sympathy. Well, Yelisei knocked at the door of the hut to get his drink of water. No one opened. He went in. He found a whole family starving, ill, filthy because no one had cared for them and they could not care for themselves. He gave them of his bread. He found his drink himself; then kindled a fire, cooked food, went out and made purchases; set the house in order, nursed the sick as best he could; the work was so much and so necessary to be done, he forgot his pilgrimage and his companion. Evening came. He could not leave. He stayed another day, and another. To leave would have meant giving these people over to death; to have left them to die in the first place would have been more merciful. Harvest was at hand. The man of the house was getting able to work now, but his field had been taken from him, his implements he had sold. Yelisei redeemed the mortgage; bought a nag and cart, and brought back the scythe. He provided some food for immediate use. All this he did, without previous intention, but feeling the necessity and yielding to what seemed God's will. Early the fifth day, before the family were awake, he took his departure.

Meanwhile Yefim had waited, and gone on, and expected at every halt to be overtaken by Yelisei. Not at Odessa, not on shipboard, not at Jerusalem, was any trace of him. Yefim visits the holy places. He goes to the chapel of the Sepulchre. Wonder of wonders! in the most privileged spot of the sacred place he seems to see his companion standing — waits for him after service, but fails to meet him or to learn anything about him. Three times this same thing happens; Yefim fails each time, and at length, his money spent, himself pretty much the same Yefim still, returns to his home; he has accomplished his pilgrimage.

Yelisei on that fifth day looked into his purse and saw he had not enough to cross the water with, much less visit Jerusalem and return. He commended himself to God's mercy, trusting sometime in the future to redeem his vow, and came back to his people.

But the story does not end here. At Yefim's home all seems to have gone wrong. A year he had been absent; his son had gone from bad to worse with drink; his affairs, though he was well-to-do, were in a distracted condition. Yelisei, on the contrary, when he comes back, is prospered in his bees and his farming as he had never been, and, content with little, this home was now in its modest abundance unboundedly happy and grateful. And this is not all. The family whom the good man saved from death knew not who the stranger was, — only that he was a pilgrim. So they sought to requite his goodness by showing kindness to all pilgrims; and also to Yefim on his return they gave hospitable entertainment, and told him their story. "If he had not come to us," said the peasant, "we should all have died in our sins. We were perishing in despair; we murmured against God and against men. But he set us on our feet; and through him we learned to know God, and we have come to believe that there are good people. Christ bless him! Before, we lived like cattle; he made us men."

Such is this story of "The Two Pilgrims," which every one ought to read. It raises the question, Which of these two made the true pilgrimage? Will not our text teach us to answer: A true pilgrimage before our God and Father is this, to visit the holy places where Christ is in the persons of His needy brethren, and to minister unto them? As one has happily paraphrased it, "The pure ritual, undefiled in God's sight, is the ritual of Christian tenderness, the activity of Christian love."

PURE RELIGION. 99

The apostle James was not one of those who belittle public worship and Church ordinances. He was a Hebrew of the Hebrews; in observance of all which the law prescribed he was so exact and scrupulous that, Christian though he was, the Jews of Jerusalem called him "the Just." He loved the Temple, with all its hallowed associations, its stately ritual; he loved the religious customs of Israel; he loved, moreover, the order and the institutions of the Christian Church. When, therefore, he says that the true worship is in the devotion of good deeds of unselfish love, we may be assured that the words are not from one who delights in standing outside the walls of the Christian Church and flinging stones at her windows. There is in the utterance nothing disdainful or cynical. He expresses himself thus because he so profoundly feels the necessity that love and good deeds should rise up continually as fragrant incense from the Christian life; because of the profound conviction that without this sacrifice no sacrifice of confession, prayer, or psalm can do God any honor at all.

And see how reasonable it is, once you give it careful thought. The public worship of God in all the various acts whereby we openly proclaim ourselves to be His has its undoubted value; and that value lies in this, that by such a proclamation we put ourselves anew on the right side, —

we again commit ourselves to all that is highest and best, at the same time that we encourage and incite others to put themselves with us under our God and Father, to honor Him by obedience; and that in a sense is what we might call the philosophy of worship, on its human side.

But by so much as words are cheaper than offerings and professions easier than their fulfilment in conduct, by so much may public worship — the ritual of the sanctuary — fall short of that other ritual of which the apostle James speaks. And the doing of those things which go to make up this ritual, this "religion pure and undefiled before our God and Father," will exert an influence like the influence of public worship, — the same in kind, but greater. A man turns out good work, or in his professional services is courteous and obliging: it is easy to say, "He does so for his own advantage." This may be the case or it may not. A man is kind to his family, his friends: it is easy to say, "It is only loving himself in another form, — it is *his* he cares for." But there are some forms of love and some good deeds which cannot fall under any such suspicion. When Yelisei spends his time and empties his purse for a family of beggared peasants whom he never saw till yesterday, and from whom he can expect no favor in return, the kindness is under no suspicion. Of such sort is "visiting the fatherless and widows." The expression had become proverbial in Israel; it signified doing good to those who could urge no claim and hold out no inducement of reward. This was charity, mercy, love unadulterated; this was kindness, pure and simple, — not like so much of giving of presents and bestowing of favors, which expects an equivalent sooner or later. Such as this our Lord had in mind when He said: "When thou makest a dinner or a supper, call not thy friends, nor thy brethren, nor thy kinsmen, nor thy neighbors, lest haply they also bid thee again, and a recompense be made thee. But when thou makest a feast, bid the poor, the maimed, the lame, the blind; and thou shalt be blessed, because they have not wherewith to recompense thee."

You say such things will be very rare. I do not deny it. Just in that degree do they stand out clear and significant. There may be shallow worldlings who will say that the man who would do thus must be a fool. Let the world say what it pleases, the man's witness will still be seen and heard.

"How far that little candle throws his beam!
So shines a good deed in a naughty world."

And wherever it shines it is a testimony to the presence of a Power that can compel such forget fulness of self and make sacrifice sweet. It is a testimony of loyalty to another and higher idea than that of the world's opinion or a base self-interest; it is a testimony of the worthiness and lovableness of that God who can inspire such loyalty and retain such a hold on the affections and the life. A man may speak the noble words of the creed of Christendom in the service of the sanctuary; but in good deeds like those he utters *the thing itself* in action louder than words, — his faith and trust in the Eternal, whom he loves and serves, and whose he is. The one may be nothing more than saying, "Lord, Lord;" the other is "doing the will of the Father in heaven." Which will best serve to make the Father known to men? Which will be most sure to express the real meaning of a man's life? Which will most praise God?

Do you recall that excellent little story by Rose Terry Cooke, *The Deacon's Week?* The minister proposes instead of the Week of Prayer a Week of Practice. The congregation all fall in with the suggestion, except old Amos Tucker. At the end of the week, *he* has this to say: "I'd ruther go to forty-nine prayer meetin's than work at bein' good a week. I b'lieve my hope has been one of them that perish; it ha'n't worked, and I leave it behind to-day. I mean to begin honest, and it was seein' one honest Christian man fetched me round to' t." The power of pure religion and undefiled before our God and Father filled that week, and made it better, for all purposes of devotion and worship and evangelism, than the former week of prayer.

But we must not forget the apostle's second clause. "And to keep himself unspotted from the world."

The religion of Israel made much of cleansing of the person, the garments, the utensils; ceremonial washings, especially in connection with worship. And what we have said before we must repeat here, that the writer of this Scripture did not regard such ceremonial observances lightly. These ablutions he practised strictly. When therefore he warns us to attend more strictly to another kind of purity, we ought to attach the greater importance to the warning.

We may, then be *spotted*. And it is the *world* from which we receive these spots.

"In a marsh," says Robertson, "each single plant is harmless; the festering, noxious juices come out of the many." This miasma is that world of which the apostle speaks.

We all know it very well. We know a world good and beautiful, in which it is a joy to live and breathe and work: a world such as that of the 24th and the 104th Psalms. The glories of the heavenly lights, the freshness of fields and woods in spring, the sparkling surface of the blue lake, the rippling brook and stream; the honest work of head and hand, which is a joy and not a curse, in the mere doing of which there is rich reward; the happiness of home with its affection and peace and cheerful mutual self-denials; friendship's warm hand-grasp and beaming eye; the generous stirring of the love of country and the devotion to the commonwealth, which we call patriotism,— put all these together, and you have the great *good world* in the midst of which God has set us, and for which we should daily thank Him. Let us not forget that there is this good world, and that it is ours.

But neither let us forget that there is *another world*. It may seem to be the same world, but it is as different from it as day from night. It tends always to lead away from the Divine and toward the demon and the brute; down, never up. It is the miasma generated from the poison of the many. It is not particularly here, or there; it is intangible; it is in the atmosphere. It besmirches the whiteness of our sweet children, makes them familiar with things which even to know is defilement and burns like a red hot iron! It makes us false, it makes us artificial, it makes us dishonest, it makes us greedy, it makes us weak to assert what we feel to be better, it makes us strong to run after evil. Don't you know *that world?* It is its voice which says that this good thing you purpose is "impractical," "visionary." It is its voice which sneers at your aspirations: "All very well to dream about, but that is n't the sort of world we are living in." It is its power which turns magnificent gifts and opportunities aside from use for the public good, and makes pliant tools of public leaders and law makers. It is its poisonous influence which gets into us all like some horrible deadening, enervating plague, so that we sit still, and let wrongs and lies go on, and say when too hard pressed, "It cannot be otherwise in this world."

What are you going to do about it? Possibly not much; possibly not wrest any great trophy from this defiling power: but, with our eyes upon Him who also walked hourly in the midst of sin, who faced the foul Tempter in the wilderness and prevailed, and met the contradiction of sinners without yielding Truth or Right — let us say, *Myself* at least, by God's help, I will keep from lying, from cheating, or from winking at lies and cheating; *myself* at least I will respect as a child of God; *my* manhood I will not sell for any vile barter of yours nor surrender for any impotent threat! Can any Christian soul do less?

We believe we have a much better creed than Matthew Arnold's; but perhaps, according to the apostle James, Matthew Arnold has a better religion than ours when he says, of *The World's Triumphs :* —

> "So far as I conceive the world's rebuke
> To him address'd who would recast her new,
> Not from herself her fame of strength she took,
> But from their weakness who would work her rue.
>
> "'Behold,' she cries, 'so many rages lull'd,
> So many fiery spirits quite cool'd down;
> Look how so many valors, long undull'd,
> After short commerce with me, fear my frown!
>
> "'Thou too, when thou against my crimes wouldst cry,
> Let thy foreboded homage check thy tongue!'
> The world speaks well; yet might her foe reply:
> 'Are wills so weak?—then let not mine wait long!
>
> "'Hast thou so rare a poison?—let me be
> Keener to slay thee, lest thou poison me!'"

"What will you do about it?" *Guard yourself*, says the apostle. Go into it and go through it you must; just as our Blessed Lord did. No dreamy, harmless land of ease, where you may abide till life be past—God has no such country for you to dwell in. "I pray not," said Christ, "that Thou shouldst take them out of the world, but that Thou shouldst keep them from the evil one." Were these vain or idle words? If not, then give heed to them. As I have said, perhaps you cannot wrest many trophies from this world; in other words, perhaps you cannot put down many evils and wrongs, or accomplish signal reforms; but *guard yourself* you can, and Christ's prayer and God's help are with you in that.

Keep yourself unspotted from the world! But you are spotted already? Alas, who is not? Well, scarred-let us come into the kingdom, since otherwise it cannot be; stained with those old stains of the past, but, by God's grace, not with any more like them from this day forth. Mark what I say. The world may take those Commandments of God and add its nullifying clause to each, and call its revision Public Opinion, or Fashion, or Political Platform, or Business, or what not: what have you to do with that? Study Christ's example. What *He* needed to avoid, so as not to spot Himself, that it would hardly be safe for you to have much to do with. Especially what He tells you in so many words to abstain from, that shun. With most constant care and earnest effort you may again and again be betrayed. You may err and fall; but it will be vastly different from the too common spotting and soiling of Christians' characters and lives; men will see that you have some decent regard for the high and holy things you profess, and they will honor you, your faith, and your God.

VIII.

The Price and the Purchase.

Knowing that ye were redeemed, not with corruptible things, with silver or gold, from your vain manner of life handed down from your fathers; but with precious blood, as of a lamb without blemish and without spot, even the blood of Christ.—1 PETER i. 18, 19.

VIII

THE PRICE AND THE PURCHASE.

GOOD Friday! It is the day on which holy quiet, and meditation joined with prayer, were fittest, could our Puritan people but cast off the strange feeling that such observance was disloyalty to great principles. Singular and lamentable misconception!—when all the world is preparing to celebrate His victory with every emblem of gladness, that it should be perchance of doubtful propriety for Christians to commemorate that victory's awful cost! From the world, it is true, we need expect no encouragement to such observance. The day will not lend itself to display or to easy enjoyment; its lessons are too searching, its scenes too overwhelming, to afford topics for light chat and complacent after-comment; its appropriate service must be, of all in the year, freest from the things which the worldly mind can feast upon and discuss. No, it is not a day the world will bid us keep! For us, however, unto whom He is precious, are not the lines of Keble true, who asks, —

> " Is it not strange, the darkest hour
> That ever dawn'd on sinful earth
> Should touch the heart with softer power
> For comfort, than an Angel's mirth ? "

But how shall we worthily speak of that great Sacrifice? For there can be, we feel, but one theme to-day, The Meaning of the Cross.

The very spirit of the occasion will help us to approach it aright. At other times we might be easily led to discuss it as a theological proposition; but when we bring before ourselves the very scenes through which our suffering Saviour moved, the mocking and the scourging, the disciple's denial, the insults of the leaders, the hooting of the mob, the way of the cross, the fainting under the woeful burden, the ignominy of the criminals on either side, the agony, the thirst, the darkness, the expiring cry,— then to reduce it all to an abstraction, and deal with it in controversy or even in merely intellectual dissertation seems nothing less than sacrilegious. Verily it was not for this He suffered and died, that we might spin fine theories, and exhibit our philosophical acumen, and strive with our brethren over words to no profit! The reading of these last chapters of our Gospels will speedily recall us to the reality of the great Sacrifice which we have done so much to hide behind our formulas. Let the day bring us face to face with the *Fact* of the offering, remembering that this is what our souls need, this is what humanity needs, this will glorify Him who was lifted up on the accursed tree.

At first sight it might appear that the text we have taken from Saint Peter was precisely such as would not lead us to the Fact, but rather furnish us with a doctrine concerning the Fact. Closer attention will convince us, however, that the whole aim and purpose of the apostle's writing is practical; that he is endeavoring not so much to inculcate sound views as to bring us to right attitude and right conduct. In keeping with that purpose he lays hold of this most solemn matter of the death of Christ, not on the theoretical side, but altogether on the fact side: "Ye were redeemed with precious blood, as of a lamb without blemish and without spot, even the blood of Christ." It is as if he had said: "If ye are in anything better men than ye were, it cost Jesus Christ His life to secure it. Live accordingly, then; in grateful obedience acknowledging the debt, and willing to be entirely His."

The price and the purchase, — this is the great truth which we would once more bring home to ourselves. We are well aware of a popular repugnance to all that looks like a commercial presentation of the Atonement, and we confess we share it; but we feel equally certain that there is nothing essentially degrading to the sacrifice of our Lord when we regard it as a price He paid.

The soldier leaves his family, the comforts of his home, and the profits of his business that he may serve his country's cause; he yields his life on the field of battle, or with more tedious suffering in the crowded hospital; he lays down his life as a price, and we deem it honorable to view it in that light. The physician, in a time of epidemic, when the community is panic-stricken, and the baser instinct of men is to flee as for their lives, remains at his post, goes from bedside to bedside, stoops over the dying, and breathes the poison, works day and night that he may relieve and save where it is possible, and finally is himself carried off by the disease: his life, too, we regard as a price nobly paid. A young priest sees an island filling up with a population of lepers. Cut off from all society save of their fellow-sufferers, having bid farewell to their friends, they are cast into that grave of living death, doomed, and yet compelled perhaps for years to linger on earth; the young priest is moved with compassion, bids farewell to the world, goes in health to take up his abode among that dying people, to share their life and bring them what comfort he may for body and soul; he becomes, as was inevitable, a leper himself, and in the course of a few years dies as his fellows are dying: Father Damien pays his life as a price.

A price, — that is, simply, the payment of what secures the desired object. The national life is threatened, the national liberty is at stake, — will be lost except patriotism respond and make prompt offering; the soldier's life then is the price, and the national life or the national liberty is the purchase. This is no theory; this is simple fact. Moreover it is not an atrocious transaction. "Sweet," said the pagan poet, "is it to die for native land." Or the health, perhaps the very life of the community is imperilled by the invasion of the plague; men, women, and children will die by scores and hundreds unless prompt measures are taken and thorough-going effective treatment be at once applied; the physician's life then, which he takes in his hands as he goes in and out and does the work of six men and forgets himself because of the terrible need, — that is the price; and lives saved and the disease stamped out are the purchase. Again not theory, but simple fact, whereby his memory is cherished as that of one who was an honor to his profession, a lover of mankind. And Molokai, — it had been, without Father Damien, a hell on earth. No law, no restraint, the anarchy of despair, the beastliness natural to those who had been cast off like corpses from the presence of the living, the hopeless horror of continued existence which was not life, — before it could be changed so that there might be some comfort of human companionship, some order to protect the more helpless, some ministration to the needs of body and soul, there had to be one willing to leave his life, to make absolute sacrifice of it. Father Damien's life was the price paid for humanized Molokai.

Note one thing more: just as the patriot's, the physician's, the leper-priest's sacrifice commands the reverence of all right-thinking men, the full approval of reason and conscience, when the object is a sufficient one, so, on the other hand, the transaction is belittled before our moral judgment when the object is inadequate. The soldier who dies for conquest or "glory," the physician who should die for the lack of wise precaution or from boastful recklessness, or the minister who should go among the lepers (if you could conceive it), for the sake of notoriety, and lose his life, would be throwing himself away, and would not be entitled to honor. Waste is not sacrifice. Price demands for its spending an equivalent; the purchase must be a worthy one, or the transaction cannot even win our respect,

— so thoroughly, deeply ethical is this principle of sacrifice wherever applied.

Now, our Lord Jesus deliberately entered upon a course, consciously and intentionally pursued a course, which He from the first could expect, and more and more could clearly see, would lead to violent death, if He persisted in it. "No man had power to take it from Him." Indeed, no true sacrifice can be exacted. He saw the invaded land, the plague-smitten city, the leper island, and He saw also that deliverance was possible if the price of deliverance were paid; and He paid it, — yes, He paid it, not in theology, but in actual fact. Think of it, I pray you, on the fact side! Let it be not less real a girding up of energies, an arousal of holy love, a resolute going forth, than the leper-priest's sacrifice shows us. No matter about differing theories of atonement, expiation, propitiation, and all that, which have troubled you so much; let them pass. Is it not a simple glorious *fact* that when our Blessed Lord saw the woe of humanity He resolutely went forth to put His life into the work of deliverance, and that He laid down the life, and that in consequence deliverance was achieved?

If this be so in fact, why then should there be so much protest against the presentation of our Lord's sacrifice as the price of our salvation?

For two reasons: —

In the first place, because sometimes the purchase is so represented that we cannot regard it as a worthy one. If that sinless life of the Son of God was laid down to purchase for men in some way exemption from the pain and penalty of sin, — a sort of immunity from the consequences of their evil-doing, if that was the great and central object for which He endured even the cross, then — we say it out of very reverence — then was too great a price paid for the thing obtained. It is as if a mother in daily tender solicitude sacrificed herself for her boy wearing herself out for him, at last by one final effort breaking herself down and yielding up her life, in order that he might suffer no discomfort, have every wish gratified, be spared all pain and suffering, and whenever he had done wrong might escape the bitter consequences. That might be a fond mother, but scarcely a wise one; and her sacrifice would command little respect, seeing it only served to pamper the child, whom she should have trained to manhood. Thus it is that by a low conception of what salvation is, the very sacrifice of our Redeemer is belittled and degraded.

But if, on the other hand, by His doing what He did all His life long, and at last supremely on Calvary, — if by this sacrifice He should somehow make sure man's renunciation of sin, should break the bondage, should bring out of the prison-

THE PRICE AND THE PURCHASE. 119

house a people of slaves and make them a nation of holy freedmen, whose numbers should swell age after age, whose freedom should grow more perfect year after year, then the purchase might justify the price. Reason and conscience fall down in reverence before such sacrifice.

And is not that substantially what Saint Peter suggests in the striking phrase, "redeemed from your vain manner of life handed down from your fathers"? A wrong life, a perverted life, waiting to be righted; an empty life waiting to be filled; a life maintained in vanity from the terribly tenacious force of habit, yet nevertheless to be revolutionized, — that is a great, a sufficient, undertaking, before which all mere human effort and sacrifice must stand helpless and dumb; it demanded a mightier.

"O loving wisdom of my God!
  When all was sin and shame,
A second Adam to the fight,
  And to the rescue came.

"O generous love! that He who smote
  In Man for man the foe
The double agony in Man
  For man should undergo;

"And in the garden secretly,
  And on the cross on high,
Should teach His brethren, and inspire
  To suffer and to die."

And here we may recur to the illustration of the mother's sacrifice. Let her do all she can do, let her withhold nothing, let her spend herself, lay down her very life, — always supposing that her end cannot be attained by less, — but let her do it to make a man of her son, to win him from every evil influence, to strengthen in him every good principle, to bring him daily into closer and closer accord with her own high aims till he shall see with her eyes and be filled even with that same spirit of sacrifice which possesses her; when the process has reached *that* point, all her sacrifice stands clearly vindicated and justified.

So is it with the sacrifice of Christ. The price purchases not merely this poor recruit of to-day, and that unstable, immature disciple with yet so much to be rid of and so much to gain; the purchase is of men and women *like Him*. Like Him we are to become, when all His work in us has had its full operation, when the process is complete, — then shall He indeed see of the travail of His soul and be satisfied. Not only in respect of purity from sin, but in this very capacity of sacrifice, we are to become like Him; and when the sacrifice of Him has issued in the sacrifice in us, — the very image and pattern of the Lamb of God reproduced in ourselves, — then it will appear that there was highest reason in the payment of the price.

THE PRICE AND THE PURCHASE. 121

But perhaps the protest against calling our Lord's sacrifice a price is due still more to a supposed implication that that price is exacted by God. In answer to that there is far more to be said than we now have opportunity to say.

And first, again, let us hold to the fact-side of this high and holy transaction; let us remember that the theories by which men seek to explain facts philosophically are quite distinct and separate things from the facts themselves. We are, as it were, gazing upon Calvary to-day. Let us not descend from that sacred height.

"Is the price paid to God?" Aside from human pictures of a Deity to be appeased, which let us shut out, is there anything to shock us in so regarding it? As a matter of fact, men must lay down their lives to save and help their fellows, in manifold ways; is it any shock to our moral sense to think of their paying the price to God,— that, in other words, the necessity for sacrifice is Divine, granted certain conditions? Nay, is not this the sweetness of sacrifice, that what we first received from God that we return to Him of our own accord? Or is the love which is the root of sacrifice, man-originated? No; let us remember the prayer of Saint Augustine, "Grant what Thou askest, then ask what Thou wilt." Though God did exact the sacrifice, is not He the Source of sacrifice, the Fountain of love? Is it not the very joy of sonship to come to the Father bringing what attests the oneness by which we are His? Where, then, though the Father asked the price of the well-beloved Son, — where is the "cruelty," and the "vengefulness?"

In any case, has not the fact that the sacrifice was for deliverance from sin, not for deliverance from punishment, set the whole matter in a different light? Not to satisfy the King's offended Majesty, not to placate His wrath, but to restore the lost sons of men to Himself and to their true selves, does He give His only begotten Son to a life which was daily sacrifice, but sacrifice in which that Son rejoiced!

We are told of a religious picture in a certain city in Germany, in which God is represented as shooting wrathful arrows down on sinners, Christ as intercepting and breaking them. Ethically, that God is lower in the scale than that Christ. Charles Kingsley emphasizes this glorious truth, that it was God in Christ that offered sacrifice for man, when he says, "If it was not God, if it was a human Christ, or the human in Christ, then are we left with man better than God!" God is in truth that Love that offers Itself upon the cross!

But there we touch mystery so deep that we recoil — mystery, not in that it contradicts what we know and have elsewhere seen, but mystery in that we cannot fathom, cannot conceive the Infinity which breaks upon us of what is loveliest, highest, truest as we find it, a little of it, in man! Sacrifice, is it not everywhere? Is it not the very crown of human life? Was it not because in this He was complete, that to Him was given the Name that is above every name? And what if that great Reality ran through the eternities, was somehow in the very heart and bosom of the Eternal? For saith not the Apocalypse that "the Lamb was slain from the foundation of the world"? If this be so eternal a principle, must it not be that "if He be lifted up He will draw all men unto Him"?

Oh that we could be more content to let the Cross simply preach for itself; to set forth, on our part, first and chiefly, the Fact of the Sacrifice, the actual not the philosophical Price and Purchase! Thus exhibited, the supreme characteristic of our Lord's life from its very beginning, manifested in increasing power until it culminates on Calvary — who will refuse to fall down before "the Lamb that taketh away the sin of the world"?

Unto Him that loveth us, and loosed us from our sins by His blood; and He made us to be a kingdom, to be priests unto His God and Father; to Him be the glory and the dominion forever and ever. Amen.

IX.

An Easter Summons.

Wherefore he saith,—

"Awake, thou that sleepest,
And arise from the dead,
And Christ shall shine upon thee."

EPHESIANS v. 14.

IX.

AN EASTER SUMMONS.

WHENCE the apostle takes this quotation we do not know. The words are not from the Old Testament Scripture, nor can we trace them to any apocryphal writing. It is therefore commonly supposed that we have here a stanza from an early Christian hymn; and both the form and the spirit of the lines accord well with such a supposition. They have in them the ring of an inspiring song, such as we might expect to have been sung by disciples in those days of the first great enthusiasm.

We have chosen these words for an Easter text, because, while they have no special reference to Our Lord's rising from the dead, nor to our own, they point, in a way, to the substantial meaning of all resurrection. And what is the meaning of resurrection? Simply this, we take it: the rising out of an old, partial, worn-out life into a new, vigorous, and larger life. Whatever else it may mean for us to have "this earthly house dissolved" and "enter into an heavenly," clearly it does mean a rising out of the old, partial, worn-out life of earth, into one new, vigorous, and vastly larger in a spirit-world. Must it not be that when we emerge into the light of that glorious day, we shall feel as those awaking out of sleep? With the pulse-beat of that life so full and strong, will it not seem as if the earth-life itself had been death? "Resurrection" in the Christian sense means surely as much as that.

But these words quoted by Saint Paul, —

"Awake, thou that sleepest,
And arise from the dead,
And Christ shall shine upon thee,"

are evidently for immediate, mundane application. Spoken to the living, not the dying, for the present, not some future, near or remote, they necessarily refer to something other than literal resurrection, — plainly, some *figurative* resurrection; only we do not like the expression "figurative," because that leaves in many minds the thought that it is "not real." We might call it a *spiritual* resurrection; but there again the objection arises that to many people a "spiritual" resurrection will mean as little as a "figurative" one; "spiritual," alas! is too commonly held synonymous with "shadowy" and "unsubstantial." Let us venture, then, to call it — without claiming to have hit upon the exactly fitting

AN EASTER SUMMONS. 129

phrase — *a moral resurrection;* at all events, it is a resurrection which is to take place with us here and now, and for which, it appears, we are ourselves held responsible.

And let us see if we may not make plain to ourselves, from our own experiences and observations, the force of Saint Paul's appeal.

In the history of every man and woman there are epochs. In some lives there are more than in others; in some they crowd more closely and follow more nearly upon each other; in some they make a far more decided break, lift up character to a far higher level, and more suddenly, — or, alas! more quickly and sharply turn it downward into a course of ruin. But be that as it may, in every life there are epochs. We may, perhaps, on reaching years of reflection, look back and see epochs in our younger days, places where a former stage was definitely abandoned, another definitely entered upon. Or, perhaps not so definitely, but more gradually, and yet quite as certainly. The even tenor of our way is, indeed, at no period so steadily and undisturbedly maintained as an outside looker-on might think; within, as we all could testify of ourselves, are turns, conflicts, upheavals, enlargements of view and purpose, changes of feeling, — movements, transitions, in a word, *epochs*. Remain as we are, we cannot, if we would.

"Within," we say; but obviously, also without. The child is for several years at home, with his parents, with his playmates, — his sole occupation now, to grow, like a fair young plant, "in sun and shower;" yet even there, in life's early morning, there is something of routine and discipline. The course of days, and the different parts of the day, with what belongs to each in turn — it is all more or less clearly defined in his child-mind. That is his world; in that he lives, and as yet in no other. But he is now five, six, seven years old; he is sent to school. He enters a new world. The routine is in most respects the same; the day remains divided as before; but more is put into a day. The new world is a larger world. The boy is part now of a larger order; he has things to do which rest on him with a new sense of responsibility; he learns facts and truths which reveal a realm that a few months since had no existence for him, and he has new things to think about and to dream of, new things to desire. It is an epoch passed; he has risen into an intenser life. And mark this: when he has fairly come into that life, although it may not be altogether free from what is distasteful to him, he has as natural a feeling in it as a short time ago he had in his world of toys and of Mother Goose.

This is but a single example of what life means,

from beginning to end. Out of the school into the workshop, the office, the training for a profession; that is to say, again, into a larger and more serious life, and therefore a truer and more noble, from which no manly youth could return to his former habits and occupations without doing violence to what is best in him. And then, coming out into the world, entering the struggle, shifting for one's self, held accountable, perhaps, for a family; the sort of responsibility that comes with manhood, what we might call the final pushing out of the craft upon the open sea; this itself is a new life indeed, and how much larger! and because a larger, a truer, and a better; and no one worthy of the name of *man* would prefer to leave it, hardships and all, to return to the former, more easy and less responsible.

Now in all these we have instances of a sort of *moral resurrection.* Before one enters on such a new stage he is, to the reality of the things in that new life, as it were "asleep," — as it were "dead." For some of the most constant factors and experiences in it are to him, as yet, as if they were not. And if that is true of the more outward course of these lives of ours, how much more of their inner, their inmost!

Some of us recall epochs in our religious life. There was a time, earliest of all, of little prayers learned, mere words and forms, because we could not then have understood, had they been explained. Questions arose, were asked, were answered as best they could be; and we learned the meaning of some things in our prayers, and somewhat the meaning of Him to whom, unseen, these prayers were spoken. Perhaps after that, coming away from a mother's leadings, we fell under more direct, explicit teaching, and learned new truths regarding God, His will, His works, His administration of the world. Still further on we arrived at a point where the personal question confronted us individually: how shall we set ourselves in a right relation, outwardly as well as within, toward Almighty God, His people, His Church? And we took the step, one memorable day, the first and necessary step to that great end. But still on we went; our views of that relation of God to us-ward and of ourselves to Him underwent a change, — it grew larger, more real, sweeter, — and yet we are going on; this world of Divine relations in which we live, and which we sometimes call the "kingdom of God," it stretches out farther and farther on every hand, its horizon is boundless, there is nothing with which it has not to do; it is a most real world, a most intensely living world. Gazing around us now upon this great world, this large life so full of God, we could almost say that till we lived in the thoughts and purposes and pursuits in which we now live, we slept, yea, we were dead. Thus by successive epochs have we been brought into newer and larger worlds, worlds full of things of which, in previous stages, we had no thought or conception at all.

And, if we are able sincerely to give any such account of progress in our inner life, — thanking God for it, even while we humbly confess how far we yet fall short, how ofttimes we have failed to walk by that which we had attained, — can we not also bear joyous witness to another fact; can we not truthfully say that "Christ hath shined upon us"? Nor can we conceive it to be possible for any man to pass through a moral resurrection, and take life more seriously, entering into larger and more absorbing relations with humanity and with God, without the illumination of heavenly light falling upon his pathway and flooding his atmosphere! Could it be otherwise, except perhaps temporarily, momentarily, — could it be otherwise, and God remain God? Here is the secret of that joy, to the world so unreasonable and so unaccountable, which makes its possessors rejoice in tribulation and distress. Life in its Divine largeness is to them so radiant that all the accumulation of earth's woes is too small to hide the heavenly beauty.

Take the case of the very man from whose pen came the words of our text. Saul of Tarsus was a youth with most promising opportunities, with good friends of high standing, whose influence would go far to secure him a bright future, a brilliant career. You know his story. His epoch of epochs was on the Damascus road. The summons came; he heeded it. He chose the new life, the larger life, and took it with all it involved, thoroughly in earnest, withholding nothing. It happened to mean to him persecutions, buffetings, stripes, hungerings, vigils, imprisonments, shipwreck, — at last the executioner's sword; it meant, while his body was dragged through these things, that his sensibilities should be oftentimes even more keenly wounded, his heart burdened and sore with anxiety for the churches. How think you he would have answered the man that had asked, "O Paul, was not that a mistake on your part when you threw aside the opportunities that were yours in youth, to make yourself the spokesman of an unpopular cause?" He would have answered, with perhaps even greater vehemence than when he wrote to the Philippians, "For Christ Jesus my Lord I suffered the loss of all things, and do count them but dung, that I may know Him, and the power of His resurrection, and the fellowship of His sufferings, becoming conformed unto His death!" And if one should still ask, "Did he choose wisely?" we can only make reply, that all depends upon the conception you have formed of the purpose of life; but if *the effectiveness of life, in beneficent achievement for humanity,* be a supremely manly aim, Saint Paul chose aright, and the result justifies him. The thing, however, which concerns us here and now is this: that having heeded the summons, while as yet the result of his toil and sacrifice could not be in evidence, God granted him the radiance of a heavenly Presence which no earthly storm or darkness could put by; "Christ shined upon him," giving him the support of a constant, unfailing joy!

And is there anything that men need more than this? How much the blame for unhappiness and failure is cast upon the outward circumstances of life. If but one or other obstacle could be removed, if but this or that thing could be changed, how all would go well! Some "do not get the help they should in their own home;" some are "burdened with poor health;" some are "hampered by dependent and shiftless or vicious connections;" some are "in callings in which there is no chance for one to be honest and make a living;" some are "in an atmosphere of godlessness, where to remain pure and religious is impossible;" some "did not have the advantages they ought when younger, and now it is too late;"

some are "so situated they cannot live up to their own better aims;" some are "so driven with business they cannot care properly for their spiritual interests;" some are "so absorbed in the round of social duties they cannot find time to consider the obligations of a larger humanity," — so runs the endlessly varied yet monotonous arraignment of circumstances which predestine their unfortunate victims, it is believed, to unhappiness and defeat. Sometimes the thing is spoken out, oftener it is confessed only to the secret self, and suggested perhaps by the tell-tale countenance, hungry and dissatisfied; but withal, the question still is, Who will brighten life for us? How may the joy which is more than pleasures, more than successes, more than wealth, which is mightier than troubles, disappointments, want, — how may the joy which can subsist in every environment be attained? Or is there none; is it all a delusion?

Many have said so in the bitterness of their hearts. Far be it from us to make light of any human woe, or to seek with cheap words to brush away the tremendous reality of the things that are against us. And yet we must bear our witness! We should be untrue to the glorious record of heroic souls in every age from the beginning; untrue to the noble company of faithful men and women facing, all about us, difficulties surely not less than yours, and achieving victory for both righteousness and joy; untrue even to what we ourselves have known of Divine uplift over the roughness of painful ways and the seeming insuperableness of barriers and obstacles, — untrue if we did not make haste to say, The things that be against us are not too mighty to be overcome! If our eyes could but be opened to see the whole scene, we should behold, as did Elisha's servant, the forces of the Almighty, greater than our combined enemies, ready to our help in the struggle. Truly, the thing we most need is the vision!

Fancy yourself standing at night upon that favorite spot from which you love to view the country round. Look about you,— darkness on every side, with nothing distinguishable but some dim outlines of deeper blackness. Clouds cover the sky, neither moon nor stars are visible; nothing of cheer but the scattered lights in distant windows, beckoning you to leave this gloom. Suppose there were with you some stranger to these parts, who should say, "A most dismal, dreary, monotonous country this, without a touch of variety or beauty to relieve it!" Would you not say: "Withhold your judgment, good friend, till you have seen it"? You would ask him to return when the night was gone, and the sun in the heavens, to look once more. There, spread out with almost the grandeur of ocean, but softer and not so stern, lies the great lake, a deeper blue than the sky above it, fresh, sparkling, with here and there its white-caps, and an occasional sail filling with the wind. Let the eye run along the great reach of waters to where, many miles distant, the wooded points enclose a charming bay; and now, turn and follow the sweep of woods, and hills, with dark lines of intervening valleys and ravines, hills upon hills; and on the topmost against the sky, solid forest or great single trees in striking loneliness, as if standing guard. And nearer, on the right hand and on the left of the winding road, lie fields and meadows, vineyards bursting out with warm pink buds and soft, uncurling leaves upon their ruddy wood, farm houses, and the distant village with its spires. And while you are looking, you hear a sweet note, and you turn to see a flash of blue, lost a moment and again a moment seen, — truly a most dismal, dreary, monotonous country! Is there not variety and beauty enough now? And if you should come again, adding the hearty midsummer view, and later the rich and deep autumnal coloring; if you should see it all upon a hazy day, upon a rainy day, or in winter, with the etching-like distinctness of every line; would you not begin to find it interesting? *There is enough in the place; all it wants is to be seen; let the light shine upon it, and then open your eyes!*

Is it not even so with our lives? There is enough in them, — or can be, easily can be; only let the light shine upon them! The charm will not come, the glory and the joy, by removing this or the other painful or disagreeable incident, but by bathing it all in that heavenly radiance. Do not permit yourself to deny the glory of the day because thus far you have lived in darkness yourself.

> "Awake, thou that sleepest,
> And arise from the dead,
> And Christ shall shine upon thee!"

Whether "Christian" or not, you are *asleep* just so far as your soul is not aroused to the noblest and highest interests of life, — just so far as you indolently, drowsily, let those higher claims call to you in vain. You are *dead*, whether "Christian" or not, just so far as your soul does not live in those things which are above, where Christ is. If your time and strength, your thoughts and affections, have been absorbed in pursuing the gratification of the lower man, in the traffic and hollow pleasure of earth, it matters little whether you are numbered among "Christians" or not, you are, in the heart of you, more asleep than awake, more dead than alive; and you need this Easter summons, you need a great resurrection, entered on with all the might of undivided self-committal, of earnest resolution and devout prayer; you need for your life the same purpose and aim and outlook which Saint Paul had in his. Drowse on no longer; live no more this empty death-in-life, — come forth! From this day let your existence mean more for God, for your fellow-man, and for yourself. Live the life that is real; and in the joy of that life Christ shall indeed shine upon you.

X.

Our Ascended Lord.

Wherefore He saith, —

"When He ascended on high, He led captivity captive,
And gave gifts unto men."

(Now this, "He ascended," what is it but that He also descended into the lower parts. of the earth? He that descended is the same also that ascended far above all the heavens, that He might fill all things.) — EPHESIANS iv. 8–10.

X.

OUR ASCENDED LORD.

AS Easter is the decisive victory of our Lord over him that had the power of death, so Ascension may be taken as the Triumph celebrating His victory and the end of His conflict.

> "Lift up your heads, O ye gates;
> And be ye lift up, ye everlasting doors;
> And the King of glory shall come in.
> Who is this King of glory?
> The Lord strong and mighty,
> The Lord mighty in battle!"

The battle-field at the close of the fight is not the fittest place or time to celebrate. The cruel work is yet too fresh, the thoughts are not yet calm, the meaning of it all is not yet clear; there are wounds to dress, the forces are all to be brought together and their present condition to be thoroughly ascertained; and to make an occasion of celebration all it should be, there is needed the festive array, and the gathering of glad spectators, — the friends whom the victory has benefited, has saved.

It is, of course, possible to carry analogy too far; yet some such meaning we believe we may see in that last of a succession of visible appearances of the risen Christ to His disciples, when, after once more setting forth all the meaning of His person, His work, His sacrifice, His victory, giving them His authoritative commission unto all nations, declaring His power in heaven and earth, He was taken up, and a cloud received Him out of their sight. And thus, if it were only to cheer and strengthen us in the fight in which we are still engaged, if only to renew our confidence in the Victor, who shall lead us to victory too, it would be of great profit to us to assemble during one brief hour upon every Ascension Day to get, if I might say so, new fighting courage for the life-long warfare.

But there are other lessons to be learned, more precious and more needful still. Jesus Christ brought God down to men; that is the Incarnation. But He also lifted men up to God; that is the Ascension. In Him Divinity entered earth; but in Him also humanity entered heaven. He that came down to men is the same that has gone up to God, — both in Himself, "Mediator between God and man, Himself the Man Christ Jesus." *Came down; went up*, — not stood midway, neither coming nor going, as abstract dogma often leaves Him. Note also, in passing, that a mediator perfectly such involves the fullest participation in both positions. By being perfectly

Divine, and coming down and becoming perfectly human, and returning in triumphant humanity to heaven, so is He truly become our Mediator.

"He that descended is the same also that ascended." Think what that means. Descended to the human life; descended to poverty and drudgery; descended to the limitations and deprivations of an humble home in an obscure village; descended to temptation by the Evil One, and to painful contact with the wickedness of sin; descended to controversy with bigotry, and ₁persecution by the religious leaders of the day; descended to being an outcast from "society" and to rejection by the masses; descended to betrayal by His friend, to insults by a brutal soldiery, to fiendish torture, and an ignominious, excruciating death; descended even to the realm of departed spirits, — into the underworld, "the lower parts of the earth," — came He not far enough down? Blessed Descension for men! — for He came down to where anybody could approach Him. Poor people, sick people, little children, people in all sorts of trouble, bad people, the most miserable woman of the streets whom no one else would touch, — they could all come to Him and take His time and strength. Nobody needed to be afraid of Him; nobody was afraid of Him. Sometimes the disciples would warn people off; Jesus never. "And He that descended is the same that ascended."

Consider what that means, or ought to mean, to us. It means that what He was here He is there; that what men could ask of Him here they can ask of Him there.

Do you remember that charming story of "Little Lord Fauntleroy"? How the little boy went across the sea, to a strange country, there to be an earl, and come into possession of wealth and honors, all so different from what he had known here? And when he had gone, his friend, Mr. Hobbs, used to sit and look at the place where the little boy had sat in his store, and think how strange and wonderful it was that one who was so great now should really have been with him here on those familiar terms. And somehow, being an earl, and belonging to the aristocracy, seemed quite different to Mr. Hobbs now that he had a friend there; he no longer felt so far removed from it. He wanted to know more about it, and to understand what sort of life an earl led, and so to keep near his little friend in his thoughts, and, in a sense, to live with Fauntleroy, — to live in spirit in an English castle, while his body was still in the humble shop. But the beautiful part of it was that Fauntleroy was the same there that he had been here. He was just as generous and unselfish; he did not forget his friends whom the world regarded as so far below him; he was never ashamed of them, and was just as ready to serve them as he had ever been. When he had been poor himself he had given them the best he had; and now that he was rich and powerful he still gave them his best, — the same in the castle that he had been in the grocer's shop!

May not this story, as a little parable, teach us in a humble way of Him who descended, the same also that ascended? "Having then a great High Priest, who hath passed through the heavens, Jesus, the Son of God — one that hath been in all points tempted like as we are, yet without sin, — let us therefore draw near with boldness unto the throne of grace, that we may receive mercy, and may find grace to help us in time of need."

Look at it again. "Now this, 'He ascended,' what is it but that He also descended into the lower parts of the earth?" Does it mean, He could not have been exalted if He had not first stooped down in such humility, and been beneath all, and servant of all? That is precisely what it means.

For His ascension is by law. There is nothing magical, nothing arbitrary in it. "Behoved it not the Christ to suffer these things and to enter into His glory?" Yes, you say, because God had so ordained it. I reply that God ordained it so because so it was right; and we cannot conceive of God as a Moral Being and ordaining anything different. It is the Devil who offers all the kingdoms of the world in exchange for a single act of homage; God can give glory only after glory is righteously due, thrones and kingdoms after they are earned. And the law to which we see Christ subject is the law to which we ourselves are subject; that we may know what it is to live up fully to the law under which we live, He descends to us and lives under it, and lives fully up to it Himself.

For consider. Does not the very word *triumph* imply *victory*? Does not the very word *victory* again imply *conflict*? Is that a glorious triumph which celebrates an easy victory? Can a cheap prize be a great prize? If the thing has cost nothing, if into the struggle have entered no hazards of life and limb, no wounds and pains, no desperate and almost superhuman exertions, what is it you are celebrating? Saint Paul, at any rate, made no such mistake as we are daily guilty of. From the day that the Ascended Lord appeared to him and chose him to the blessed service, he held himself to the conditions of true discipleship, which are the conditions, and the only conditions, of the Christian's final triumph. Not otherwise than the Master Himself did he expect to enter the everlasting doors. The same who bade his youthful fellow-worker "fight the good fight," "endure hardship as a good soldier of Jesus Christ," could at the close of life say of himself, "I have fought the good fight, I have finished the course, I have kept the faith; henceforth there is laid up for me the crown of righteousness, which the Lord, the righteous Judge, shall give to me at that day." And, as if again to repeat and to emphasize that in this he is not singular, that the same fight, and the same course, and the same crown are for all, upon the self-same conditions, he adds, "And not only to me, but also to all them that have loved His appearing."

No, there is nothing magical, nothing arbitrary in any of the Divine operations, in any of the awards bestowed by the hand of God. There is a righteous order by which, as God is God, all these things come in their right time and place. This Ascension, which to-day we celebrate, could have come to none other than Jesus; because none other than Jesus righteously achieved it. Let us add, it could not come to Jesus Himself until He had achieved it.

If you could conceive of Jesus' yielding to the Tempter in the desert; or afterward, to the popular solicitation to head a temporal movement; or after that, to the pleadings of His family to retire to His home and withdraw from so dangerous a course; or later, in the agony of the garden, omitting His "Thy will be done" and refusing the cup; or upon the very last day, up the steep of Calvary, crying out, "I cannot," and retracting His claims, to save His life, — if, I say, you could conceive of Jesus' yielding up His cause, sacrificing His fidelity at any one of these points, or even at some less vital moment and in some less important thing breaking down and proving untrue, all would have been defeated, and His Name would never have become that "only Name under heaven" of which Saint Peter testified, that Name which God exalted above every other for universal adoration.

And the Son of Man Himself taught us that the disciple is not above his Master, nor the servant above his Lord. What right have we to change that? What right, for the sake of a mawkish humility, or of a barren notion of Divine grace, to "leave it all to Him," when He bids us take up our cross and follow Him? We have too much flattered ourselves with sweet phrases and fond conceits, trusting that somehow the everlasting doors that swung open to Him only after the most desperate fight was finished, will swing open to us at the mere mention of His Name. Ah! not so. For what is He Captain but to lead us into battle; for what is He Victor, but that He might put into our hands the trusty weapon and show us how to wield it; for what did He endure, but that He might teach and impart to us of His own endurance; in a word, for what did He fight and afterward truly ascend, but that He might bring us to glory on the like glorious terms?

Yes, "this 'He ascended,' what is it but that He also descended into the lower parts of the earth? He that descended is the same also that ascended far above all heavens." You cannot have one without the other. God's law is fixed; as far as you are willing to descend, so far will He make you rise. We all are eager to rise; we wonder and murmur because we do not. But the reason could not be plainer. We cannot ascend except we have first descended; and we are not willing to descend. We give small, grudging sacrifices; we get small satisfactions out of them. We empty a little of self out of our lives, and admit a little of God's Spirit into them, but oh, how little! We intermit our efforts, we deviate from the right course, we leave off fighting and let the adversary have his way, — and all the time we comfort ourselves with the reflection that we are on the road to heaven! There is a verse in Scripture about being "saved so as by fire," with all one's life-building lying in ashes on the ground, and nothing to show for all the years of earthly opportunity; but that is hardly Saint Paul's conception of going home to glory!

Jesus was exalted to the right hand of God, when He had suffered the worst that earth could do; when He had emptied Himself fully, given Himself utterly for His brethren. When you and I do the same we can be where He is. You think there is only one place at the right hand of God? What, then, is the right hand of God? Is it in far off space, a throne beside the great white throne of God Himself? If that were what it meant, what would become of the closing words of our text, in which the apostle tells us that "He ascended far above all heavens, *that He might fill all things*"? No, if the heaven of heavens cannot contain the Almighty, neither can they circumscribe the place at His right hand. God's right hand is God's glorious acting Power; and to be there is indeed to be in the way of filling all things. To be at His right hand is to be in the thick of every battle, with victory pledged; to be in the midst of every good work, with success assured; it is to have God's power, and to use it, everywhere.

And how we all crave real power! We want our plans to issue in actions; we would have our words move men; we would be of the forces that shape life and conduct. Now we may have power — God's own power — and use it with telling effect every day; we, too, may be at God's right hand; but we must be willing to pay the price. "The lower part of the earth," "far above all heavens;" "emptied of self," "filled with all the fulness of God;" "made of no reputation," "having the Name that is above every name:"—this is the law of the kingdom, which our Lord fulfilled, and now would teach us, His disciples. This is the way of His cross, in which sign alone we conquer.

And if it seem a strange thing that we should speak of our ascending to God's right hand *now*, remember that this is precisely what Saint Paul himself bids us do. Indeed, unless we do so ascend now, we cannot, in the more glorious and final manner, ascend hereafter.

"O God, the King of glory, who hast exalted Thine only Son Jesus Christ with great triumph, we beseech Thee, leave us not comfortless; but send to us Thy Holy Ghost to comfort us, and exalt us unto the same place whither our Saviour Christ has gone before; who liveth and reigneth with Thee and the Holy Ghost, one God, world without end. Amen."

XI.

The Spirit of Pentecost.

Being therefore by the right hand of God exalted, and having received of the Father the promise of the Holy Ghost, He hath poured forth this which ye see and hear.
— ACTS ii. 33.

XI.

THE SPIRIT OF PENTECOST.

THE Day of Pentecost is fully come. Its great event, which transformed the Jewish Feast of Weeks into a crowning feast of the Christian Year, marks the highest summit of the achievement of our Lord. We have followed His history from birth to manhood, through the public ministry with its experience of the world's bitter unreasoning opposition, through Gethsemane and the brutal scenes of the sham trial, even to that lowest depth of the crucifixion between two malefactors; we have mourned with the scattered disciples; we have been gladdened at the triumph over death on the first day of the week; we have, with the eleven, caught glimpses of the familiar Friend, — whose familiarity, however, is now changed into something not less benevolent, but strangely exalted, so that sometimes He seems the same Jesus, and again appears as One out of another world; we have, moreover, stood gazing after the ascended Lord, rejoicing that, enthroned in glory, He is the same sympathizing Friend and Brother still; and, now that all this has once more passed in review before us, the single picture left upon our minds is of *The Man Christ Jesus*, with all that went to make up a perfect humanity, dwelling in light and blessedness evermore.

True as the picture is we need to remember that it does not exhibit the whole truth of our Lord's life. The apostle Paul indicates to us that there is something still beyond: "Even though we have known Christ after the flesh, yet now we know Him so no more." There is yet one step further for us to follow our Lord's career, strange as it may seem to say it, after the Ascension scene, — one step without which the work had been left incomplete, without which the kingdom of God could never triumph in the earth. There are, to be sure, those who would rest the work of Christianity on the influence of the example of the Perfect Man, — who would know Him only after the flesh, who would perpetuate a Christ without a Pentecost, and would simply by the beauty of that self-denying life and martyr-death win others to copy after Him; but Christ Himself is against them. Throughout the tender and solemn discourse of the evening before His death His thought leads the sorrowing disciples on to the expectation of comfort and guidance and power in an abiding Presence, which shall follow His departure. He carries forward the work begun at Bethlehem and continued even to Calvary until its completion on the Day of Pentecost. He does not rest content with deliverance from earthly griefs and ills and triumph over earthly and infernal foes; no, not till, "being by the right hand of God exalted, and having received of the Father the promise of the Holy Ghost, He hath poured forth this which ye see and hear."

Consider the glory of that day. Hitherto fugitive from their persecutors, locked perhaps (as we know they were on one occasion) within the room for fear of the Jews; not one of them, with the possible exception of Saint John, but had fled from the Lord at the critical hour; a small band with nothing in themselves to give confidence, and the visible presence of the Master forever withdrawn, — so the eventful morning finds them. While they are there, "all together in one place, . . . suddenly there came from heaven a sound as of the rushing of a mighty wind, and it filled all the house where they were sitting. And there appeared unto them tongues parting asunder, like as of fire, and it sat upon each one of them. And they were all filled with the Holy Spirit, and began to speak with other tongues, as the Spirit gave them utterance." The time was opportune. Power from above is given these witnesses just when they can bear their testimony before representatives of the entire known world. "Men from every nation under heaven" throng the place, and are amazed at what they see and hear. The sneers of a few incredulous and hostile are easily refuted. And it is no slight proof of the Divine source of this inspiration that under it the Apostle Peter, with every faculty under perfect control and all his powers at his command, stands up and pours forth no ranting, incoherent exhortation, but a clear, convincing, masterly discourse, reaching the hearts and consciences of the multitude before him. He holds up Jesus as the Messiah of their nation and the Lord of all men, — this same Jesus whom the Jews had wickedly slain. One finds it hard to recognize in him the same man that had, less than two months before, thrice denied his Lord. But this is now the day of new things; forever and decisively "old things are passed away;" it is the day of triumph, as of the Master so also of the disciple. On this same day there are three thousand asking to be baptized into the name of Christ; and the little band of disciples now swelled into an aggressive army is sealed as *the Church*, imperishable, invincible.

Let us seek to understand these things, if in a measure we may. Put with the words of our text the declarations of Christ Himself in His last discourse. One object of the mission of the

Comforter is "that He may be with the disciples forever," — "that they may not be left orphans," as Jesus so tenderly expressed it; another is "that He may teach them all things," or, in another form, "that He may lead them into all truth;" another still is "that He may testify of Christ," and "may convict the world in respect of sin, and of righteousness, and of judgment." Take also some of the statements in the Epistles, — for example, where Saint Paul calls the Holy Spirit "the Spirit of Jesus Christ," and again, "Now, the Lord is the Spirit," and in various places speaks of the Holy Spirit indwelling in the believer and in the whole body of the faithful, the Church. Saint Peter also speaks of the "Spirit of Christ;" and Saint John, in his Gospel narrative, tells us that in Jesus' lifetime "the Spirit was not yet [given] because Jesus was not yet glorified." We adduce all these Scriptures in order that we may arrive at some clearer view of what this coming of the Holy Spirit means, — that we may come out of the vagueness and confusion which surround this part of our Christian faith more than perhaps any other, and that the Spirit of Pentecost may be more real to us in our daily life. What, then, do we learn from them?

First, that Pentecost could come only after the life and death and resurrection and ascension of

Jesus. All these events must necessarily precede the great visitation we celebrate to-day.

This truth is, perhaps, not perfectly obvious. Our Lord's own word was, "If I go not away, the Comforter will not come unto you." Why not? Because before His death there could be no Witness of the Christ; the Christ had not yet become fully the Christ our Saviour. Such He was approved through His death and resurrection; for "it behooved the Christ to suffer these things and to enter into His glory;" because, we may say further, the Spirit was to convict the world of sin, of righteousness, and of judgment; and this conviction must be wrought by reference at every point to Christ, the world's Holy One and Saviour from sin, the world's perfect God-approved Model of righteousness, the world's appointed Judge.

Or, to state the same truths in still simpler form: the whole career of Jesus embraces not a single arbitrary feature; there is an organic and necessary connection of each several part with the whole, so that we cannot conceive of anything in it being shifted out of its place without displacing all that follows. Once for all let us rid ourselves of the thought of an arbitrary God, who gives or withholds, prevents or brings to pass, without reason, by pure fiat. Such a conception is daily working great havoc in the practical lives of men and women, and obscuring some of the most blessed facts of the Gospel, throwing around them an air of unreality. Each following step dependent on that which went before, — this was the law of the Saviour's life, as it is the law of every life, since God is God.

The second lesson we would seek to understand from these Scriptures is that Jesus "received of the Father the promise of the Holy Ghost." How may we interpret this to our thought?

We might, of course, look for chapter and verse where such a promise is recorded, and having found it, might suppose we had answered the whole question. Perhaps with Saint Peter and his hearers the mere reference to prophecy sufficed. We venture to suggest that to-day something more is needed. Men will ask, Why the promise? what is its significance? what necessary relation is there between what Jesus was and did and such a promise of the Holy Ghost?

Now, we think there are hints to furnish us at least some helpful suggestions in the way of answers to these questions. Let us look more closely at the subject.

Our Lord had, in His farewell discourse, told His disciples that He would make request of the

Father, who should give them another "Comforter." Note the Apostle's striking language in our text, — " having received . . . He hath poured forth." The figure is of the Father giving the gift to Christ, and of Christ in turn giving it in all its abundance to the disciples. To be sure, this is only a figure; but the truth so pictured must be not less real and striking than the figure.

And we must bear in mind again what we have already urged, that Pentecost could not come till all the preceding events in Christ's career had been past. Then we may begin to see why in all the world's history no one else could be a Saviour to man. If what man needs to be saved from is *sin*, if sin is to be vanquished and completely overmastered, — sin, and not the consequence or penalty of sin, primarily, — then the meaning of the Christ's life breaks upon us with new power. If there is or can be any Deliverer, He must not Himself be under sin's dominion in any degree. Step by step, keeping Himself pure, standing blameless, meeting and repelling every temptation, bearing every pain inflicted by the foe, faithful to the uttermost, sinning the while not even in word or thought, meeting death itself, if need be, and not overcome of sin even then: He who will do this shall be pronounced Victor over sin, — at least in His own Person and for Himself. Is there any name on the roll of humanity, save One, that has earned this distinction ?

Victor for Himself; but how about His brethren ? If His example could encourage them to a like attempt, the experiment would too soon show them how little it was in them of their own strength to wage this fight. Thank God for all that followed Calvary! What preceded would have sufficed to exalt Him forever as the Hero of mankind; what followed sealed Him as humanity's Saviour. For in the resurrection and ascension He was given back, as it were, to the sons of men, to lead them on in the great conflict to a like certain victory ; and on Pentecost began the mighty equipment, and the world-wide war which shall not cease till He hath made His enemies His footstool.

How different all lesser saviours, — if in an infinitely humbler sense we can use the term thus, — all other benefactors of man! Take any one among them, the noblest you can find ; in a career of great self-sacrifice, let us say, he has wrought out blessings for his fellows; but are there not many points in his career where the test breaks down, many things in his character which are far from perfect, and which in other characters, again, are far more nobly developed ? For a random example take the remarkable personality of Socrates. Those who have read his memoirs written by Xenophon, know that with all his nobleness he was far from being a perfect man. In comparison with such as that of Jesus his character breaks down at every step. So would that of any other of the sons of men that ever lived upon our earth. No perfect chain — no, not even one perfect link! There is no salvation for us in men.

But when Jesus, linking sinless to-days to sinless yesterdays in one golden chain, had made His whole life perfect from Bethlehem to Calvary, the plain language of Scripture shows us that God secured all the rest. "Him God raised up;" "Him He exalted to His own right hand;" for Him He gave "the promise of the Holy Ghost," — and all this, *because what Jesus now was, God could own and could perpetuate.*

Men of science tell us there is a law of "the survival of the fittest." Now we know that a law is simply a way of God's working. And we know that in the moral world, the world of spirit, His way of working is in keeping with His own character,— as Matthew Arnold says, a Power not ourselves that makes for righteousness; in other words, by the law of God righteousness is to survive.

But mankind presents at the very first glance a perverted, abnormal aspect. It is not by following out what men *now* are that this righteousness and perfection can be attained, for themselves or for the race.

If there could be a better Type of man, if men could be made over into the likeness of that better, then God's law would favor the survival of that better humanity.

And men of science also tell us of ideals in the evolution of man. They tell us that "in human evolution spirit or character is transformed by its own ideals." All, therefore, depends upon our having, not only worthy, lofty ideals, but the Absolute and Perfect Ideal.

Are we not beginning to see what is meant by Jesus' "receiving the promise of the Father?" Not to an imperfect Jesus could have been given the power to perpetuate Himself in mankind. Not to an imperfect Jesus could have been given the final prerogative of humanity's Absolute Ideal.

Now read these two verses: —

"And I will pray the Father and He shall give you another 'Comforter,' that He may be with you forever;" and, —

"No longer I, but Christ liveth in me."

Bind them together by this third: —

"But ye are not in the flesh, but in the spirit, if so be that the Spirit of God dwelleth in you. But if any man hath not the Spirit of Christ, he is none of His."

The presence of the Holy Spirit, then, is, as we may say, only the continued presence of our Saviour Jesus Christ, now glorified, not limited by time or space. Jesus in the flesh could be in but one place at one time; now, by the Father's granted promise, He can be with us all and evermore.

But even this is not the first and most helpful aspect of the truth. Is it not to simple hearts a great joy to find that the Holy Ghost, so often named in Holy Scripture, so often regarded with perplexity and awe, is but the Spirit of Christ? The same ineffable love, the same tender sympathy, the same affectionate concern for the welfare of every child of man, is characteristic of the Spirit as of that Jesus whom from the Gospels you know after the flesh,—nay, in all these Jesus was but bringing the Father's inmost Heart to human view, and revealing the Father's Character; and thus we see how these Three, the Father, the Son, and the Holy Ghost, are One, God blessed forever!

And now, since Pentecost, "the Spirit of God lies all about the spirit of man like a mighty sea, ready to rush in at the smallest chink in the walls that shut Him out from His own!" What more do we need than unfailing diligence not to hinder, thwart, deny room to this Spirit of grace? No need for a second Pentecost. Oh, the unbelief of

THE SPIRIT OF PENTECOST. 169

supposing that there is very little of God's Spirit present among us!

Yes, let us henceforth have done with these barren, joyless Christian lives! Not only the honest effort, the sense of duty, but the fulness, the largeness, the liberty, the spontaneity which lift us up, do we want. Surely we all have somewhat of that Spirit, feeling the influence of His presence in that little measure in which we surrender ourselves to Him. But let us henceforth *surrender ourselves wholly to Him;* let our joy be full; let peace richly abound, the peace of being no longer at cross-purposes within; let us do with great gladness all we do in Christ's name,— it is our privilege; let us live full lives, not starved, sickly, half-dead, not dragging ourselves on from task to task with listless knees; let us surrender ourselves wholly to Him, that He may sanctify us wholly; 'tis easier to live out-and-out for God than to try to serve two masters; let us surrender to Him the citadel of the heart, that He may drive away every enemy of the consecrated life!

And if any consideration could move us to make such a surrender, should it not be this, that He is altogether on our side? We read of "the Comforter," and elsewhere of "the Advocate" and "the Paraclete;" but why not say at once, "the Helper"? *The Helper*— that is the precise force, if not the exact translation of the word.

The Holy Ghost our Helper; sent to be always near us, always ready to respond to our call, always prepared to take our part, always willing to rescue and guide, always allying His strength with our weakness.

> "Closer is He than breathing,
> Nearer than hands and feet."

Looking at it in its length and breadth, surely we may say that with this truth of a Spirit of Pentecost life becomes a very different thing; we may join with the Apostle in the glad exclamation: "The old things are passed away; behold, they are become new!"

XII.

Contending for the Faith.

Beloved, while I was giving all diligence to write unto you of our common salvation, I was constrained to write unto you exhorting you to contend earnestly for the faith which was once for all delivered unto the saints. — JUDE 3.

XII.

CONTENDING FOR THE FAITH.

NO utterance, at the present moment, could well be more opportune. Men seem to be thoroughly confused as to the great matter of Belief: some panic-stricken and desperate, others threatened with chronic scepticism and ready to throw all positive faiths overboard. Never was there greater need of instruction in first principles; and what these are we think may be easily discovered by giving careful attention to this Scripture. The writer of our text holds the key to the situation.

There are, obviously, two principal inquiries to be answered, if the exhortation is to have due weight; and when they have been answered, and the answers have been well pondered, we are confident that very much besides will have been made clear: first, *What is this faith which was once for all delivered unto the saints?* secondly, *How shall we to best effect contend earnestly for it?*

If we would make any progress toward an answer of this first question, our minds must be cleared of notions derived from a state of things utterly unknown in Jude's day; we must bring back the plain meaning of words in his age, rid of all later accretions. To be sure, there is no startling novelty in this advice; yet the method is so rarely followed by either our heated defenders of orthodoxy or our self-complacent agnostic critics, that one may be permitted, in the name of common-sense, to recall everybody to its necessity. Let us, then, carefully attend to the words, and we shall already be a long way toward a clear understanding of the whole matter. What "faith" is this? The faith held by Jude, and by the Christian people whom Jude addressed; the first-century faith, not the fifth-century, nor the sixteenth-century. In the bare recollection of this one fact there is much to help us. But the writer characterizes it further as "once for all delivered unto the saints." If "once for all," then evidently he has never known any other, does not contemplate the possibility of any other in the future. It is the first faith. While he states that it was "delivered unto the saints,"—that is, according to the common New Testament usage, "to the Christians,"—he omits to state by whom it was delivered. He deems that unnecessary. There was but one company of men that had a faith to deliver to the world; we agree in calling them

Apostles. The question therefore reduces itself to this: *What, in point of fact, did the Apostles bring to the world as the Christian faith?*

Saint John introduces his first Epistle with the statement, "That which we have seen and heard declare we unto you." Evidently he regarded it as *testimony*. He and his associates had been chosen to receive immediate and personal knowledge of a Great Fact, of which in due time they were to be the witnesses. There is less than no reason to think that they were indoctrinated in a theology, or schooled in a system; those are structures which man may always be depended on to rear for himself. No; but by the intimacy of several years' companionship, by the interpretation of life's deeper meanings in the light of the Divine Fatherhood and of the true Sonship, by the unceasing marvel and glory of His own high purpose and unremitting strong devotion to His God-given work, shining forth through gentle and unassuming meekness; and afterward by the fearful night in Gethsemane and afternoon on Golgotha, followed by the sorrow, the hopelessness, the restored joy, the new light, the exultation in powers before unknown, — by these experiences, all clustering about His own Person, Jesus prepared His chosen disciples to go into all the world speaking of "what they had seen and heard."

Take now your New Testament, and turn to the Book of Acts. Read again the account, so full of life and movement, of how the Apostles went forth, and how and what they wrought. Attend specially to the discourses, and note the form in which these first Christian preachers deliver their message. I know of no better way to satisfy ourselves at first hand of what those men understood to be "the faith." Prepared, as we have said, to witness of Jesus Christ, they did so witness, before Jews and Gentiles. They told their story. Varying in order and in relative prominence of details, sometimes more emphasis here, sometimes more there, yet the story is the same story over and over again: that Jesus was come into the world, the Son of God, to be our Lord and Saviour, that He went about doing good, approved in mighty works, delivered into the hand of Pilate and crucified by the Jews, on the third day raised from the dead, ascended to glory, blessing His disciples with the gift of His Spirit, offering remission of sins to all who would repent, believe, and be baptized in His Name. There was as yet no single "form of sound words," the convenience of what we might term a "portable statement;" that was to come later. But it was "the faith," a plain, simple and single thing to accept at the Apostles' word, and requiring no erudition or acuteness or profundity to master; accepted on Pentecost day by the three thousand who had listened to Saint Peter's preaching, and soon after, in city after city, in Europe and Africa as well as Asia. That this account of Jesus as the Christ should in the course of time be put into concise form, perhaps in the first instance in connection with the baptismal profession required of the candidate, was natural and inevitable. Thus the Churches obtained their creeds, which, by natural assimilation, merged in a few centuries in the form of the so-called "Apostles' Creed." When thus developed, the significance of this symbol is not in its constituent articles as a series of theological propositions (as if you must take them one by one, accept or reject), but in its entirety as a current and admirable summary of "the faith" delivered by the Apostles. And at the present time, aside from the claims of its venerable beauty, there is a very practical fitness in rehearsing this creed as a part of every divine service.

As to creeds, so-called, there are many; and yet *there is no creed but one*. There are not many faiths delivered; there is "the faith once for all delivered;" by which token we may satisfy ourselves that, so far as creeds (so-called) oppose each other, — negative each other, stand each upon the erroneousness or dangerous defectiveness of others, finding material for assertions in their rivals' denials, and for denials in their rivals' assertions, — so far are they *not* statements of "the faith which was once for all delivered unto the saints." Doubtless they have their necessary place in the onward march of theological thought; but they are misnamed "creeds." A doctrinal compendium is not a creed. The creed occupies itself with the testified fact of Jesus as the Christ; not with controverted opinions, chiefly metaphysical. Therefore, if a man would be a Christian, he must accept the creed, not for the creed's sake, but the faith's which it plainly sums up. Phrase that faith in other or better words if you think you can do so; as to the things themselves which are rehearsed, it is not for us to add to or to take from them; thus was it from the first delivered by the witnesses. Try the witnesses anew if you will, — sift their testimony, reject it altogether if you must; but remember that the net result in your hands is not what the apostolic Church understood by the Christian faith. Clear and definite, single and distinct, *that* still stands challenging the world, — the same to-day that it was eighteen hundred years ago.

But, such being this faith, how shall we contend earnestly for it?

Not chiefly by polemic and apology, the weapons of theological science; for the articles of the faith are not less moral than historical. Taking that faith in its germinal form, "Thou art the Christ, the Son of the Living God," — how would one believe that and contend earnestly for it? "Flesh and blood hath not revealed it unto thee, but My Father which is in heaven," was Christ's reply to His disciple's confession. To believe in Jesus was at least as much a matter of spiritual penetration and insight as to believe in a friend, a leader, a cause. It meant to perceive and adore the innermost Jesus; and this was not for the worldling, the frivolous, the covetous, the hypocrite. A hundred men might see this Jesus go in and out among them just as the believing disciple did, might hear Him say all He had to say, look on as He wrought works of mercy, — some would call Him "a gluttonous man and a wine-bibber, friend of publicans and sinners;" others, "the carpenter, the son of Mary, — whence hath *he* these things?" others, "Elijah," or "one of the prophets." But, in the face of all that, Simon Peter, with that God-given insight, beheld the glory of Jesus' strength and purity and love, was convinced that He was right, and that if the whole world differed from Him the whole world was wrong, — evidently a state of mind far in advance of the mere recognition of Jesus as the Messiah of the prophets, proven to his Hebrew intellect.

And you and I repeat Saint Peter's words, confessing that we believe in Jesus as the Christ. Do we truly so believe? Do we believe in Him so much that we should follow in His way against the dissuasions of the world, to our own temporal loss? Or, if He were to appear among us to-day in guise corresponding to that of the Nazarene carpenter of old, should we then believe that to none other could we go, — He had the words of eternal life? Searching question for us all! But in Jesus Christ we say we do believe. Do we, then? "Lord, I believe; help Thou mine unbelief."

Suppose, then, the beginning of a true believing is in us, though it were but as a grain of mustard seed, how shall we contend earnestly for it? By being on our guard that no man take it from us; by entering into its inner meaning more and more; by endeavoring to see all things in Jesus' light; by binding our affections and aspirations into one with that principle which made Jesus' life *single*, — the principle of being ever about our Father's business; by living our whole lives thereby, repulsing temptation and opposition, and sacrificing no part of it to any encroaching power.

How admirably is this truth further illustrated when we consider some of the controverted particulars in the apostolic account of Jesus; for we find in that account, and therefore in the creed, what we variously call the "miraculous," the "supernatural,"— expressions which are bungling and unsatisfactory, and yet difficult to supersede, if indeed one had any better to suggest. What shall we do with them? They are not merely secondary or incidental matters, not to be quietly dropped as non-essentials. A great field here opens to view. "Contend earnestly for the faith"? "Prove the New Testament books historically trustworthy; show the important and vital relation of this miraculous element to the narrative as a whole; vindicate it further by exhibiting its reasonableness, its antecedent probability, its sober and lofty tone,"— thus will the theological disputant begin to point us to a plan of campaign. Well, when it is all accomplished, what have we attained? We have enriched our minds by adding to our store of information certain biographical data concerning Jesus. Was it for this the Apostles bore witness? Not at all.

One and all they said, "*Repent,*"— "amend your lives;" "change your life-purpose." What had that to do with believing their testimony? Everything. The testimony had from the first this one thing in view, that they who should believe in Jesus as the Christ were to bring their life-purpose into line with the life-purpose of the

Christ. How powerfully this is unfolded when Saint Paul comes upon the scene. Could any one more strenuously insist upon the historical fact that Christ actually rose from the dead on the third day? How he asserts and defends it in that fifteenth chapter of First Corinthians! But how much more he insists upon that which our Lord's resurrection now demands of us. "If, then, ye were raised together with Christ, seek the things that are above, where Christ is, seated on the right hand of God;" "Christ being raised from the dead dieth no more. . . . Even so reckon ye also yourselves to be dead unto sin, but alive unto God in Christ Jesus." It is in a manner well enough that we should understand the historical and philosophical questions involved in the resurrection.[1] But let us never think

[1] I cannot but quote here from Frederic W. H. Myers ("Modern Essays," *Renan*). What he says in this connection has the greater weight because of his singularly untrammelled temper of mind regarding all controverted questions:—

"'Phenomena of this kind,' it is sometimes said, 'need not now be disproved, for they are disbelieved without formal disproof. Precisely so; they are disbelieved because they are traditionally supposed to be violations of natural law, and we know now that natural laws are never violated. But this argument has a flaw in it. For until such phenomena are not only disbelieved, but weighed and sifted, we cannot tell whether they are in truth violations of natural law or not.

"It can hardly be expected that the common-sense of the public will permanently accept any of the present critical

that this is our real business; it is in one sense irrelevant. If the thing had been a delusion or a lie, it would have been dead these many hundred years; but there is in some way an eternal power proceeding from that Judea of eighteen centuries ago, with its band of witnesses telling of One they had known who had died and risen again, — a power which sets the Person of Jesus apart as

explanations of the alleged appearance of Christ after death. It will not accept the view of Strauss, according to which the 'mythopœic faculty' creates a legend without an author and without a beginning; so that when Saint Paul says, 'He was seen of Cephas, then of the twelve,' he is repeating about acquaintances of his own an extraordinary assertion, which was never originated by any definite person on any definite grounds, but which somehow proved so persuasive to the very men who were best able to contradict it that they were willing to suffer death for its truth. Nor will the world be contented with the theory according to which Christ was never really killed at all, but was smuggled by some unknown disciples into the room where the Twelve sat at meat, and then disappeared unaccountably from the historic scene, after crowning a divine life with a bogus resurrection. Nor will men continue to believe — if anybody besides M. Renan believes it now — that the faithful were indeed again and again convinced that their risen Master was standing visibly among them, but thought this because there was an accidental noise, or a puff of air, or even a strange atmospheric effect! Paley's 'Evidences' is not a subtle book nor a spiritual book. But one wishes that the robust Paley with his 'twelve men of known probity' were alive again to deal with hypotheses like this. The Apostles were not so much like a British jury as Paley imagined them. But they were more like a British jury than like a parcel of hysterical monomaniacs."

unique. Our business with the resurrection is to pass on from the occurrence itself to the relation which this occurrence bears to the spiritual life of mankind, to our own spiritual life. Realizing the power of eternal life, we have the surest evidence that the beginning of it all was not in a lie, a myth, an hallucination, but in that which after all is still the simplest and most reasonable to believe, — "the third day He rose again from the dead." Lacking that evidence, we are nothing profited by cartloads of apologetics. The best way to contend for the faith of the resurrection, is to live steadfastly the risen life.

So with all the other features of a "miraculous" nature. Making them the centre of conflict is to miss their true significance. They are to be taken as organic parts of the faith once for all delivered, from which we pass on to their inner meaning and power in the new life. It is *that* which must meet the enemies of the faith, and win the fight.

Of one other article we would make particular mention, and that one of a rather different order from the preceding. The "Gospel of the Resurrection" soon passed into a Gospel of the Crucifixion. Regarding the meaning of the cross men have reasoned and speculated much. The occurrence itself affording no opening for discussion as to its historical credibility, the more did the "doctrinal" opportunity draw off the energies of men from that which concerned them more to that which concerned them less. Questions of the forensic bearings of the transaction in the court of heaven engaged men's minds to the exclusion of the power of the cross in the Christian's daily life. Part of the faith it verily is that Christ died for our sins, that He is the Lamb of God that taketh away the sins of the world. It may be well to study this great transaction critically, on its various sides, in its various bearings; but let us not for a moment suppose that this is our real business with it. Holding the faith of Him crucified is, not only to believe that Jesus of Nazareth came to His death in this manner, and that His dying thus bore some essential and mysterious relation to the counsels of Deity — which who will deny? — but rather, passing on from that, to crucify ourselves, as Saint Paul has it, we that are Christ's to crucify the flesh with the affections and lusts, always bearing about in our body the dying of the Lord Jesus. This it is, we think, to hold the faith of the Crucified. Anything less is not faith in the Crucified, but an opinion regarding the crucifixion. And to contend earnestly for this faith is not to frame and vindicate even the most profoundly philosophical theory concerning Christ's sacrifice; the foes of the faith are not intellectual, and they assail us where to be compelled to fight seems to us far less glorious, — in the motions of a heart gravitating constantly toward self-pleasing and vanity and worldly success, in the subtle temptations to neglect or slight the homely duties of every day and every place, in the thousand-fold besetments of the lower nature. He that "smites these foes by the merit of the holy cross" is the true champion of the Christian faith.

Is it not sufficiently plain, then, that this faith is after all a very simple and practical matter, — simple, as all greatest things are simple, and practical as all deepest things are practical? It was for a great moral purpose that Jude wrote this strange, brief letter, with the exhortation of our text; and it is for a great moral purpose that we ought to speak and move to-day as regards all questions of belief. This "faith once for all delivered unto the saints" is one which no one holds save he who believes it true for himself, and in himself, and in all things he does, or plans, or meditates; it is a faith for which no man earnestly contends save he who really holds it with the constant struggle of the world in his heart to make him only think or only say it; who will not be deceived into thinking that that may be true in his theology which is but partially true in his religion, or that what is true in his religion must not be too hard pressed in this practical world. To make this faith tell, to bring things to pass in our time and in our surroundings by the power of it, to get God's name hallowed, to make His kingdom come and get His will done on earth as it is in heaven, by virtue of believing in Him whom the Father sent, — this is to contend earnestly for it.

In the light of so urgent business in so great a cause, what becomes of our hot contentions of this present, over matters ranging in importance from the secondary to the infinitesimally trivial?

Does not the foundation stand sure? Is not Jesus Christ the same yesterday, to-day, and forever? And the once delivered faith — is it not Himself? And is there any way to contend for Him at all, save by being true to Him?

"But ye beloved," Jude continues, "building up yourselves on your most holy faith, praying in the Holy Spirit, keep yourselves in the love of God, looking for the mercy of our Lord Jesus Christ, unto eternal life."

Grant this, O Lord, unto us all. AMEN.

THE END.

www.ingramcontent.com/pod-product-compliance
Lightning Source LLC
Chambersburg PA
CBHW032148160426
43197CB00008B/824